PARSNIPS, BUTTERED

D0813020

LANCASHIRE COUNTY LIBRARY

3011813628831 7

PARSNIPS, BUTTERED

BY JOE LYCETT

Hodder & Stoughton Ltd
Carmelite House
50 Victoria Embankment
London EC4Y 0DZ

www.hodder.co.uk

HODDER

First published in Great Britain in 2016 by
Hodder & Stoughton
An Hachette UK company

1

First published in paperback in 2017

Copyright © Joe Lycett 2016

The right of Joe Lycett to be identified as the Author of the Work has been
asserted by him in accordance with the Copyright, Designs and Patents Act 1988.

All rights reserved. No part of this publication may be reproduced, stored in a
retrieval system, or transmitted, in any form or by any means without the prior
written permission of the publisher, nor be otherwise circulated in any form of
binding or cover other than that in which it is published and without a similar
condition being imposed on the subsequent purchaser.

A CIP catalogue record for this title is available from the British Library

ISBN 978 1 473 64043 6

Typeset in Sabon MT by Palimpsest Book Production Limited,
Falkirk, Stirlingshire

Printed and bound by Clays Ltd, St Ives plc

Hodder & Stoughton policy is to use papers that are natural, renewable and
recyclable products and made from wood grown in sustainable forests. The
logging and manufacturing processes are expected to conform to the
environmental regulations of the country of origin.

LANCASHIRE COUNTY LIBRARY	
3011813628831 7	
Askews & Holts	13-Feb-2018
828.9202 LYC	£8.99
NTH	

CONTENTS

ABOUT THE AUTHOR

On 5 July 1988, a potent mix of viscous liquids coalesced and became known as Joe Lycett. Joe Lycett is found around ponds and marshes in the West Midlands of the United Kingdom. The specific origins of Joe Lycett are not known but, based on the duration of an average pregnancy and taking into account menstrual cycles, it is likely he began around 7 October 1987, just as the movie *Fatal Attraction* was arousing audiences across the Western world.

Soon after his conception, presumably as news spread that a foetal Joe Lycett was blossoming in his mother's womb, the Black Monday financial crash of 19 October 1987 devastated the markets, with the Dow Jones falling a massive 508 points. This was just the beginning of a lifetime of global financial disruption and massive amounts of parking fines.

Around 7,000 days passed and the young Joe Lycett was now a not-so-young Joe Lycett. He had decided to take on the institutions. He became livid when he realised that his local bus company in Birmingham was one of the only bus companies in the UK to not give change to its customers. Irate at this discovery, he launched a brilliantly titled campaign called 'Time for Change', which culminated in just under 200 likes on Facebook and a meeting with the bus company's PR team. Despite a passionate plea to their common decency, the campaign was a failure, Joe bought a car and he forgot about the whole thing.

But this desire to improve the world in small but important ways lived on, and Joe has since become well known for campaigning for what some would call 'pointless matters' but which he actually thinks are 'very important' and 'What do you know, Dad? Why shouldn't I send a knob of butter to every Topman store in the UK? You can't stop me.'

He is known as a 'comic' (*Guardian*), 'young' (*Time Out*), 'relaxed' (*The Times*), 'messy' (*His Mother*), 'not famous enough to abandon my date' (*Someone on Twitter*), 'not funny, annoying face and voice' (*Someone Commenting on The LAD Bible*).

He has appeared on BBC Radio 4 on *Just a Minute* and *Loose Ends*, and is the host of panel show *It's Not What You Know*. His television credits include *Live at the Apollo, 8 Out of 10 Cats Does Countdown, Sunday Night at the Palladium* and *Would I Lie To You?* and he has served ice creams at the Palace Theatre, Manchester, and Alexandra Theatre, Birmingham. He would like you to know that the spoon is in the fucking lid. Have another look. No, not under the lid, in the lid. Look. Yes, it is there. I told you. Don't take that tone with me, just because I'm on minimum wage doesn't mean I'm an idiot.

He leaves behind a mother, father and sister – he's not dead* but he often leaves them in coffee shops, despite promising to give them a lift home.

---

* *Accurate on publication. He may well be dead by the time you read this and would like you to know that the afterlife is a nightmare beyond any human comprehension.*

The first sentence of the paperback of your first book is the most important sentence you will ever write in your entire life.

Helen Lycett, my mother

INTRODUCTION

To find your dirty prostitute's name take your mother's surname and put her first name in front of it. How do you like THAT for an opening line, Mother.

Life is hard. We are a bombarded generation: there's Twitter, Instagram, taxes, newspapers, adverts for balding, the Panama Papers, watches that read your pulse, terrorism, gluten-free bread ... There's such an onslaught to the senses these days it's a marvel any of us manage to get out of bed. God I love bed.

Whilst we are overwhelmed and confused by this miasmic cloud of information, there are those who seek to take advantage: there are parking fines, hate tweets, email scams and Christmas newsletters from old school friends about their ugly kids. And just as we get round to doing something about it, we're distracted again – Sandra from head office has emailed to ask why we've started using Kenco Millicano when it's three times as expensive as Aldi own-brand instant coffee and no one can taste the difference. Well, Sandra, it's mainly because when I drink the Aldi stuff I get the shits. Also: get a life, Sandra.

I, Joe Lycett, star of stage and screen, am here to help using my main weapon: mischief.

During my short life of doing largely nothing, I've discovered some unusual solutions to many of life's common problems. Other self-help books by people like Alain de Botton or Eckhart Tolle may give you tips like, 'Encourage dialogue with your partner by asking them regularly what you could do to improve' or 'Connect to your inner spirit by wearing a hemp jacket and listening to Simply Red.' I will not be imparting such profound wisdom. Nor will I be giving tips like, 'Put tack on the side of your desk to hold your laptop cables' or 'Use a clothes peg to secure your coffee and keep it fresh.' WE DON'T NEED TO KEEP THE COFFEE FRESH, SANDRA, IT'S ALDI COFFEE, IT NEVER TASTED FRESH IN THE FIRST PLACE. If you are looking for enlightenment or kitchen advice, may I suggest you look elsewhere. Also: get a life, Sandra.

No, I understand that life's problems are complicated and the solutions need to be nuanced. As such, in these pages I will impart to you advice that is 'out of the box'. By that, I mean I am sitting in a cardboard box writing this advice.

For example, here are some of my tried and tested LIFE HACKS:

LIFE HACK #538: Melt four KitKat Chunkys together with a warm knife for a fun way to forget you are crippled by loneliness.

LIFE HACK #639: Try 'Dry January'. Every time your mouth feels a little dry, fill it with gin!

LIFE HACK #205: Spice things up in the bedroom by covering your genitals in cayenne pepper.

LIFE HACK #926: Save paying to see *Fifty Shades of Grey* at the cinema by logging onto a computer and searching for 'pornography'.

LIFE HACK #284: Recreate Glastonbury Festival at home by draining your iPhone battery and pissing yourself in the garden.

LIFE HACK #285: Recreate Reading and Leeds Festivals at home by draining your iPhone battery and shitting yourself in the garden.

LIFE HACK #286: Recreate Latitude Festival at home by draining your iPhone battery and having awkward, underwhelming sex with a girl called Annabel from West London in the garden.

LIFE HACK #294: Add energy to a dinner party by saying 'what do we think about Brexit' before opening a shoebox filled with wasps.

Let me reassure you, I've tried each and every one of these tips, and they all work!*

I have been a mischief for pretty much my entire life. I've found that it actually is one of the most consistently effective ways to

---

* *They do not work.*

respond to the ridiculous rules and regulations that are so prevalent in modern living. My mantra is this: if you're going to be ridiculous with me, I'll be ridiculous with you. In fact, even if you're not being ridiculous with me, I will still probably be ridiculous with you.

If you're not sure what I mean by the ridiculousness in modern life, let me give you an example. A couple of friends of mine recently made the selfish gesture of getting married. They conducted a hideous occassion commonly known as 'a wedding', which involved an impractical dress and, most troublingly, an online gift list.

I would've bought something from the list sooner, but I was too busy researching how feasible it would be for me to have a pet pig, so when I finally came to check it on the day of the wedding all the good-looking stuff (by 'good-looking' I mean 'cheap') had already been gifted, leaving a knife set and a bin. I didn't want to be that guy who buys someone a bin, so I clicked on the knife set and began the process of entering my payment details. An alert flashed across the screen: 'The item you are buying is age-restricted, please pay with a credit card to verify your age.' I've never had a credit card because I can't be trusted not to get drunk and buy all the yoghurts in a 24-hour Tesco for a laugh, so I figured I would ring them and establish that I am a 27-year-old man in showbusiness, in order to resolve the matter.

Alas, it was not to be so simple; they informed me on the telephone that I could not purchase the knives without a credit card because they had no idea how to otherwise prove my age. A link to my Wikipedia page would apparently not suffice. I was baffled. I said to the girl, who was becoming increasingly less polite: 'Let me get this clear. You think that I am potentially a child, posing as an adult, attempting to illegally buy knives by gifting them to a couple on their wedding day?'

There was a pause.

'Yes, that is a possibility,' she replied.

I hope you liked the bin, Will and Jess!

Unfortunately, these absurd rules are becoming something of a normality. Many big companies have directives and regulations that have no discernible logic and, as such, they have become key targets of my fury. Don't get me wrong, I'm not against a lot of big companies in principle – I confess I quite enjoy the occasional Burger King Whopper or a Costa mocha – but all too often one finds certain organisations to emulate soulless, profit-obsessed psychopaths employing teenagers who don't give a shit and just follow the rules. Plus they maintain a tight grip on our town centres so that it is increasingly impossible for independent businesses to get established. But other than that, I quite like them.

One route of attack on these companies is our old friend Twitter. Most of the big multinationals have well-maintained accounts from which they appear to listen to their customers, when actually they are reading the tweets aloud in the office and laughing at them before they block you and go out for sushi. Regardless as to whether they reply, block or ignore me, I intend to continue publicly complaining and shaming them on a regular basis.

I have done much good work trolling Starbucks, a company that annoys me for a million reasons, and that claims to have good coffee when they absolutely do not have good coffee. Even Sandra doesn't touch the stuff and that's not because it is thirty-eight times more expensive than Aldi. I tweet them frequently with jibes like this:

.@StarbucksUK FYI I'm on your Starbucks 'customers only wi-fi' but I'm actually next door in Strada having a Prosecco and I don't give a shit.

Or there's my invaluable work with Cadbury, which used to be a family-run venture based in my hometown of Birmingham, before it was bought out by Kraft, who made loads of redundancies and changed the recipe of the Creme Egg. I tweet them on the regular, with stuff like this bit of guff:

.@CadburyUK Is it tru u killd da Easter bunnie wif a nife?

And finally there is this little nugget that I sent to Uber:

.@Uber My driver just farted. FIVE STARS.

This, dear reader, is just the tip of the nonsense iceberg. By the time you have finished reading this book, you will have learnt how being daft can help to:

- reverse a parking fine!
- manipulate the tabloid press!
- take a celebrity selfie!
- navigate social media!
- work in the advertising industry!
- respond to hate mail!
- send the perfect Christmas Newsletter!
- defeat ISIS!
- support football!
- call out your local MP for being a knob!
- fix the railways!

AND MUCH, MUCH MORE.

And by 'MUCH, MUCH MORE', I mean 'NOTHING MORE'!

'But Joe, what actual experience do you have?' you might ask. Let me tell you, even though that is clearly a loaded question and I don't like your attitude. I have been training for the last five years at the International Institute for Helpful Life Hacks (otherwise known as 'the Internet') and have never held down a serious job. In my life, I have spent a lot of time asleep or in the bath. Whilst this sounds like I've been doing nothing, let me assure you – this is not true! Shut up Mum, I'm writing my book! I know tons of things. I know that pelicans have three eyelids. And apparently they've removed 'gullible' from the dictionary! My friend told me that on April 1st last year!

Let me be clear – you must now keep this book on you at all times. Never let it slip from your grasp. If you follow my instructions to the letter, the hints and tips concealed within this tome will make you more powerful than you ever possibly imagined – you will rule your domain with an iron fist, crushing those around you with ease, to emerge as a supreme and formidable leader. Your name will invoke fear in thousands – women and children will run from you, even grown men will howl and shriek in terror, such will be your reputation as the greatest living human who has ever graced this sphere.

Either that or it might just be a bit of a laugh, I dunno.

Hope you enjoy it love you bye

Joe
xxxxxx

NB: This book is unlikely to provide any useful advice. If you are looking for guidance on taxes, quitting smoking, moving house, love, divorce, education, healthcare or anything actually important, may I recommend speaking to friends or family members and not consulting a book by a comedian who eats halloumi at least twice a day.

TRY TO
WRITE THE
NUMBER
6 WITH
ONE HAND
AND THE
NUMBER 8
WITH THE
OTHER.

IF YOU
CAN'T DO IT,
YOUR DAD
IS GAY.

A NOTE ON ALIASES

You will notice as you read through this book that I utilise a number of aliases. The main reason for this is to protect my identity – if you were to Google my name, it wouldn't take you long to discover that I send a lot of weird complaint emails and then the game is given away. A false name, whilst dishonest, is sometimes essential to make the point.

The other key benefit of an alias is that it allows me to go further and harder with my nuisance. I am a largely calm and untroubled man; as long as there is halloumi and high-quality ketamine available I don't want for much. Without my aliases, many of my complaints would end after the first reply stating, 'We have checked our records and can confirm you were parked illegally.' On my own, I cower at authority. With my aliases at my side, I will one day rule the world.

I find a useful way of getting into the skin of an alias is to create and update their own Facebook profile, like a psychopath might. I've only ever been accused of being a psychopath a couple of times and neither of those people have said it again. They haven't said anything again. They're dead. I killed them. Haha, only joking. I am not joking.

It starts with a simple profile, a little bit of background, a couple of friend requests. Gradually, every couple of days I will try to post something that feels in character. This behaviour has resulted in many of my friends texting me with things like, 'Who is Samantha Salamander? We're mutual friends on Facebook and she seems unhinged . . .' or 'Where did you meet Brian Pottering? He seems like a dick!' I met Brian Pottering on the travels through my mind and he told me a magical and fascinating story about how benefit cheats should be shot in the street, which I wrote down as a status update in his name.

My first alias was a gentleman called Paul Wenbridge. I had a lot of fun creating Paul; I used a picture of an obscure bodybuilder as his profile and created an appalling 'lad' personality. On the surface Paul was a cheerful if aggressive alpha male but he quickly revealed himself to be racked with anxiety and self-doubt.

Here is a short introduction to some of the aliases you are likely to encounter in my book/life. If you receive an email from one of these people, it's me.

PAUL WENBRIDGE

An absolute lad and a lost soul. Famous
for tweets such as:

> *Just had hair of the dog. Now ive got*
> *a mouth full of hair and the dog looks*
> *ridiculous LMFAO!!!!!!111*

and

> *Just did a wank on a snail lol*

I successfully convinced many of my friends that he was a real
person, albeit a horrific hypersexed idiot of a person, which
started a downward spiral of fake accounts culminating in
about sixty different email addresses and social media logins,
which I struggle to keep track of.

PAUL PAULINGTON

My most frequently used alias – Paul is a solic-
itor with no knowledge of law and a keen eye
for a news story. He's often in touch with a
tabloid newspaper and his favourite magazine
is *Chat!* He is still very upset they didn't buy
his story about how he has eight dogs (and by
dogs, he means little porcelain statues of dogs).

SAMANTHA SALAMANDER

A sultry, seductive complainer who works in Pret A Manger (she refers to it as 'la Mange') but who dreams of bigger things. Posts on her Facebook look a bit like this:

OMG Pixie Geldof just came into my la Mange!!!!! She was so nice and gave me a great tip about getting into media: 'Just get out there.' Such an exciting day, love you Pixie!!!!

NIGEL FARAGE

One of my most successful aliases, I managed to create an entire political party with him as the leader, somehow winning a seat in the EU and initiating Brexit. People are still unaware that he is actually one of my finest creations, even though it's clear that someone like him couldn't possibly exist in the real world.

ANGIE MERK

Not to be confused with the super-popular Chancellor of Germany, Angela Merkel, Angie Merk (or Angie M as she's known to friends) is a numbers girl with an eye for a good deal and a sharp full-body suit. She's most notably absolutely thrilled that Birmingham has a German Christmas market and loves a bit of *knoblauchbrot* (garlic bread).

NIGELLA FARAGE

A chef and campaigner for UKIP. She *hates* immigrants and *loves* goat massaman curry. Some of her most memorable quotes include:

If Nigel has 3 apples, and Sergey has 4 apples, then how did Sergey get into this country?

and

A Frenchman, a Romanian and a German walk into a bar. AND THAT BAR IS ENGLAND, WHICH HAS TURNED TO SHIT.

I fully expect this chapter to be used as evidence when I am sectioned.

MY FACIAL RECONSTRUCTIVE
SURGERY WENT HORRIBLY
WRONG...

... BUT I'M MANAGING
TO KEEP MY CHIN UP.

A NOTE ABOUT
THE FOX

Dearest of readers, as you peruse the pages of this book you will notice I frequently use pictures of a fox in my exchanges. You may observe that I tend to do this when I have run out of options in an email exchange or simply when I am being frivolous – you would not be wrong in this observation.

Whilst my main residence is in Birmingham, whenever I have work in London I stay with friends in a beautiful and loved old house in Peckham. The house is a sanctuary that homes all sorts of creatures, from comedians and actors to a cat called Button and now The Fox.

In my opinion The Fox is the funniest animal in residence. I can't articulate fully what it is about The Fox that I find so amusing, as it is something indescribable and intangible. An ethereal hilarity. I think it has something to do with the absurd expression he adopts when anyone walks past him, which manages to look simultaneously startled and profoundly bored. I imagine his inner monologue as he picks through a bin to be something like this: 'I wonder if there's a bit of lasagne in here today WHAT THE FUCK WAS THAT?? Oh it's a car OK no worries ooh look there's some old rice I can tr . . . WHAT THE FUCK WAS THAT?? Oh it was someone closing a door two streets away WHAT THE FUCK WAS THAT??' etc.

I do not understand why foxes have inhabited the urban environment. I concede that there's maybe more readily available food than out in the wild, but I personally find when I'm petrified of everything around me I struggle to engage fully in a meal. Although, I still manage OK in Wetherspoon's so there's always exceptions to the rule. Most urban foxes' nerves must be wrecked. Living in the city for a fox is the equivalent of a human being with a sensitive disposition setting up camp next to a grenade-testing site.

We have had a number of urban foxes take up residency in the garden over the years. Most notable was No Ears (named because he had no ears), who was in very little distress about his situation as he was clearly born without them and as such hadn't developed a complex. No Ears was a sassy creature. If anything I think his hearing was far superior, as I tried to capture him a few times and he was always the fastest. No Ears stopped appearing after I bought my crossbow.

The fox in question is simply known as 'The Fox' and started appearing at the back of the garden and gradually, over the period of twelve months or so, built up the confidence to get closer and closer to the house. There was a moment when he got about halfway down the garden and encountered the cat, Button – both stood their ground and there was a five-minute impasse which only ended when someone coughed in a garden five houses down and The Fox sprinted away as if he were being attacked by the full US military.

He now frequently resides in the porch doorway, curled up on the mat, enjoying the warmth of the house. If anyone arrives back when he is sleeping there, he waits 'til the absolute last minute to move, aiming a furious and frustrated look at them as if to say, 'Do you absolutely have to come through this door?' Then, like a lethargic teenager he crawls onto the wall at the side of the house and curls up with a resigned sigh. I'm guessing he sighs, I've never been close enough to hear it.

The reasons I have chosen to use The Fox frequently in my exchanges are because:

1) I think he's hilarious.
2) I don't have to get legal permission to use his picture.
3) Once this book is in print, I want to contact a lawyer as The Fox and see if I can sue myself for defamation.

So here, fair reader, is the beloved Fox. You will see much more of him amidst these pages. I intend to make him famous.

COUPLE IN NANDO'S HAVING A HUGE FIGHT.

I WOULDN'T NORMALLY TAKE SIDES, BUT THOSE PIRI CHIPS LOOKED TOO GOOD.

HOW TO
AVOID BEING SUED
WHILST WRITING THIS BOOK

I've wanted to write a book for as long as I can remember. I can't remember much before last Thursday, so it's probably not that long really. I thought that it would be really easy to write a book and it would be kind of like the experience JK Rowling seems to have, where you just go to coffee shops and think deeply about things for a couple of months and then suddenly you're a multibillionaire and best friends with Daniel Radcliffe.

The problem I've had is my book is not about a magic boy – unless you consider getting rid of a parking fine magical – but about a real boy, me, Joe Lycett. This book is based in the real world: within these pages are emails and exchanges with real individuals and real companies. Apparently there is this thing called The Law which stops you from doing certain things that affect people in the real world. I thought The Law was there mainly to stop people from taking drugs and ensure wealthy people retain their grip on power, but apparently it's also designed to spoil my fun.

Soon after agreeing to compile this book, I was contacted by a lawyer (these are people in wigs who understand The Law and can tell you exactly what is wrong with you for an indescribably large fee even though you can probs just Google it), who explained to me the very serious repercussions of writing the words on these pages:

Mr Lycett,
I gather the book you are writing will include some correspondence with individuals and companies. I have been asked to explain the legal rules to you around this for your reference:

1. Don't be defamatory about anyone in your letters (i.e. not only the person/company you are writing to but also third parties).

2. If you're making a complaint make sure the complaint is true – i.e. don't complain about avocados being too hard in Waitrose if they aren't actually hard!

3. Write to companies over individuals where possible.

4. Seek permission or disguise the company/individual. In some cases we will need to seek permission or change names, but that can be decided case by case.

5. Photos will need clearance as a rule – you may get away with some, but most will need permission if the owner is known.

A good rule is – if they're identifiable, you're liable. If you make every effort to hide the identities of those people you've written to, you should be fine.

Best,
Jimmy Jimjams

As you can see I've disguised the name of this lawyer by affectionately calling him 'Jimmy Jimjams'.

It appears that whilst I just thought I was having a bit of a laugh, what I'm actually doing is considered in the legal community to be akin to murder. I'd love to find myself in jail having the following conversation:

ME: *What are you in for?*
INMATE 1: *I slaughtered a family of four while they slept in their beds. How about you?*
ME: *I published a silly letter to a local council in a comedy book and didn't change the name of the person I was sending it to.*
INMATE 1: *That's tough.*
INMATE 2: *You've dropped the soap, Lycett.*

However foolish I feel The Law is, I wanted to make sure that I was fully complying with Her Majesty's Government's wishes, so I responded to Jimmy with a few follow-up questions.

Hello Jimmy,

Wow, so there's a lot to take in here. I didn't realise writing this book would throw up so

many legal issues! I just want to make sure I've got my head around everything you've sent me so I have some more questions, for clarification. My main concern is to avoid getting sued 'cause I went through that before and it cost a lot to have the guy 'removed'.

- So as far as I understand it, if I'm using emails from someone I have to either get their permission or change their name. Can I make their names into anagrams? Can I make them names of other people I don't like? Can I make all their names 'Amanda Holden'?

- Can I pretend to be someone I'm not? I've invented aliases with silly names like Paul Paulington and Samantha Salamander that I use to protect my identity when emailing some people.

- Can I pretend to be Angela Merkel on email? What if I change her name to Angie Merk?

- If I can't defame a human being and ruin their reputation, what about animals? I know a fox that I want to make famous but I'd struggle to get his permission.

- I really like the rule 'If they're identifiable, you're liable' but I don't like the rhyme. I've thought of some better ones for this. How about: 'If they're named in your tale, you're going to jail' or 'If they recognise themselves a bit, you're deep in shit.'

- I know it is illegal to draw on a banknote, but what are the legal repercussions of creating a giant origami statue out of £5 notes depicting the Queen putting her middle finger up at a newborn baby?

- What are the legal repercussions of strongly hinting in my book that anyone who has sued me in the past has been killed?

- In your professional opinion, if I wanted to have someone killed what's the best way of going about it?

- Have you ever killed anyone?
- Do you have access to a gun?
- Finally, please can I have permission to use your emails to me in my book?

Thanks,
Joe

P.S. Oh also, can I put a picture of you in my book? I want to draw a picture of a lawyer and I found a picture of you on Google from a firm that you used to work at. Hello cuteypie! I've attached what I'm thinking. I've drawn you with a pig's body to protect your identity.

I must confess I was absolutely thrilled with my drawing of Jimmy as a pig.

Hi Joe,

Let me get back to you on this.

Thanks,
Jimmy

I'm still waiting to hear. I'm guessing he's trying to source the gun.

I AM MY OWN WORST CRITIC.
AS IN, I AM NOT VERY
GOOD AT CRITICISING MYSELF.
I'M FANTASTIC, WELL DONE ME.

HOW TO
BEHAVE IN THE OFFICE

I am writing to you from a rented office space in my home town of Birmingham, a small room in which I normally write stand-up comedy and currently this book. That's all I do in here, honest. There definitely isn't a half-drunk bottle of Scotch and a bong in here. OK, I'm off my tits. I deliberately have very few 'officey'-looking things, just soft furnishings, candles and an abundance of flowers, because I believe in the methods of Elton John and it hides the smell of vomit. It's an office unit but it's not an office – more specifically the police have registered it as a 'crack den'.

The unit to the right houses a recruitment firm and I despise recruitment firms. If you've managed to avoid ever being on the books at one you are one of life's winners. I was not so fortunate, and I found the whole thing absolutely soul-crushing. The very nature of being registered with a recruitment firm means that you are openly treated like a commodity, the sum of your skills, while the fact that you are also a human is deliberately ignored. Sure, I can type thirty words a minute but I can also love.

I once got a job through a recruitment firm in a call centre, which involved me ringing up elderly and infirm people and offering them reduced price guttering and soffits. To this day I don't know what a soffit is and I'm not about to find out now. I had a script that started with, 'Is that the man/lady of the house?' You had to decipher, based on their 'hello', what gender they were and, as gender is a fluid and complex thing, I would often get it wrong. On one occasion I asked, 'Is that the lady of the house?' after which a distinctly male voice started laughing for a sarcastic amount of time before saying, 'Now fuck off.' Fair enough.

The other job I got through them was in an Aztec-themed indoor mini-golf emporium, where I served drinks and listened to the same recording of various exotic birds on loop for ten hours a day. It was fine except for the manager, who had great fears of a terrorist attack and would occasionally ring up with a fake bomb threat to test whether we knew the protocols. Because of course, terrorists are clearly thinking, 'We've done 9/11 in New York, we've done 7/7 in London – where next? Aztec-themed mini-golf.'

In most public places, when a fire or a bomb is found, something is announced in code over the tannoy along the lines of, 'Mr Sands is in the male toilets', meaning 'there's a fire in the male toilets', to avoid panic. A bomb is usually something like 'a friend of Mr Sands'. But despite being very sweet, the staff at mini-golf were a few Jägerbombs short of a vomit and so we would literally

have to say, 'Mr Bomb is at the front entrance.'
The phone calls would normally go like this:

Me: *Hello, mini-golf, how can I help?*
Caller: *There's a bomb in the mini-golf.*
Me: *Hello Brian.*
Caller: *It's not Brian. It's . . . Ahmed.*
Me: *Oh right, hello Ahmed. Where's the bomb?*
Caller: *By hole number 7.*
Me: *OK cheers, thanks for ringing.*
Me on tannoy: *Mr Bomb is on hole number 7.*

Then Brian would come out of the office to check if anyone was doing anything and find one of the staff just kind of hanging around hole 7, pretending to look for a bomb whilst also texting.

Thankfully I was only subject to the toils of the mini-golf for a short time and immediately wiped my name from the books of the recruitment firm, sparing myself a life of data entry for a small government department. But I will never forgive them for those lost years (I worked there for two and a half weeks).

To the left of my office is a PR business and there is a woman in there with a phone voice like a basketball player changing direction. Every screech and yelp of 'Darling, we'll get a centre spread in the *Birmingham Mail*' or 'We'll get it trending on Twitter' seeps through the paper-thin walls and into my brain. I wouldn't mind, but I've made such a relaxing space for myself that it's like being punched in a hot tub.

Because I hate everyone in the offices around me, I've taken to putting daft signs up on the front door. Every other week or so I'll have a different company name, a different company picture, an advertisement for something. I'll also change my wi-fi name to something stupid like 'Poo' or 'Heroin4U'. It's a sort of test to see what I can get away with and also ultimately, I suppose an attempt to make them laugh and like me.

One evening, after a couple of glasses of a terrible single malt and a toke on a phat spliff blud, I mocked up a sign that made me actually laugh out loud. I don't often laugh at myself, but I was dead chuffed with this beauty.

HAVE YOU SEEN THIS CAT?

Missing from this area.
Answers to the name of Samantha Peterson.
Any information to Peter at pppeterpppeterson@gmail.com

Yes, it's a picture of The Fox. I don't know what I was expecting to get out of it but it made me so happy to see it in my snap frame every time I came back from the loo that I didn't really care. I suppose I thought someone would send me something funny to Peter Peterson's email. No such luck.

Mr Lycett,
It has come to our attention that you have a sign for a lost cat in your office door snap frame. May I remind you that it states in your contract that we have a strict policy on animals in the building, as this is a workplace. Animals are not permitted, and anyone found with animals in their units could have their contract terminated.
Regards,
Carole
Management Assistant

I've drawn Carole to look a bit like Judy Finnigan because why not?! Ignoring the fact that Carole has completely missed that it is a picture of The Fox, I don't like her tone. And I checked the contract and it actually says nothing about pets, so she's got nothing on me.

Hello Carole,
My apologies, there has been a simple misunderstanding. There is indeed a sign for a lost cat in the snap frame but Samantha Peterson is NOT my cat.
   I am attempting to find her, as I believe she has been stealing from me. I popped into the office late one night last week and discovered that my collection of antique biscuits had been disturbed. Outside the building I spotted a cat and instinctively shouted, 'Samantha Peterson'. The cat turned, and so I deduced that is her name. I know she has my biscuits. Any help you can provide would be most appreciated.
Many thanks,
Joe Lycett

Mr Lycett,
I am sorry to hear about the disruption at
your office, but I would like to politely ask
you take the sign down. The surrounding
businesses have made complaints that their
clients are being disturbed by your sign.
Regards,
Carole

How can you be disturbed by a sign? I think Carole is bluffing.
Before I had a chance to reply, she sent me a follow-up message.

Also, can I ask what the Peter Peterson email address is on the
sign? Are you sharing the office space?
Carole

Hello Carole,
No, Peter is my private investigator.
He has agreed to live in the office and
work on this case for as long as is
necessary.
I have replaced the sign with my
compliments.
Many thanks,
Joe

I replaced it with this.

WANTED: DEAD OR ALIVE

APPROACH WITH CAUTION

Any information to Peter at pppeterpppeterson@gmail.com

Two days later, another email from our old friend Carole the 'management assistant'.

Mr Lycett,
We've had more complaints that you've
replaced the sign with a very similar sign.
Also, you can't have anyone living in your
office. Is there a time today we can we
speak on the phone? It would be easier
to discuss this rather than over email.
Regards,
Carole

Carole,
I'm afraid that will not be possible. I have
been advised by Peter Peterson that I
shouldn't use the phone as it could be
bugged.
Thanks,
Joe

OK Mr Lycett – I just had one of our security
guys go round and there is no one
answering the door and the lights appear to
be off, so I'm fairly confident your
investigator isn't living in the office.
As long as you don't have pets in the office,
I'm happy to forget the whole thing.
Regards,
Carole

Carole Carole Carole,
Of course your security man didn't spot
Peter Peterson. He is a private
investigator and shape-shifter. He lives in
the cracks. He's watching you when you
least expect it. He lives in the shadows of
your darkest fears. In your weakest
moments, when you're naked and vulnerable, he's there,
watching, waiting, protecting. He lives through all of us, within
us, beside us. He is the breath on the back of your neck, the
breeze in your hair, the moisture in the air.
Cheers,
Joe

P.S. Also FYI, I found Samantha Peterson last night. I slaughtered her as sacrifice to our beloved gods and burned the body in a tribal ceremony. I took the sign down this morning.

Thank you.
Regards,
Carole

I did put up another sign for a bit. She didn't bother me about it.

THANK YOU

Thanks to the information provided by offices on this floor this animal was captured and slaughtered. Many thanks.

I'M FEELING A LITTLE HORSE!
AND AFTER THAT I'M WANKING
OFF A PONY!
I HAVE SERIOUS PSYCHOLOGICAL
DAMAGE AND NEED URGENT CARE.

HOW TO
RESPOND TO HATE MAIL

I have been known in my time to appear on the occasional comedy panel show. And what of it? Sure, they're hardly high art but they're a very popular format in the UK and I like getting paid to be daft. Get off my back, we've all got to earn a living.

The panel show is increasingly critically maligned yet remains well-liked, perhaps because having a number of comedians on one show should offer up a comedic style for pretty much everyone. You might like a caustic wit, a rude one-liner or someone who tells a funny story. Maybe you like a super-cute blonde comedian from Birmingham with some silly letters he's written. You've got good taste. Whatever your taste, most panel shows should entertain you, at least a little. The flip side is that with an abundance of comic voices there is a higher risk that you might be forced to watch someone you don't like. You might've tuned in because you find one particular personality funny only to discover that they have to share airtime with some irritating, precocious upstart called something like Joe Lickit, who you don't find amusing in the slightest. Why have they booked this plum-voiced camp prick? Why isn't comedy like it was in the old days? What shops are open now that will sell me a bottle of Glen's Vodka? Why did Patricia leave me?

I understand this troubling predicament because my uncle texts me about it every time I am on the television.

Whereas you or I might switch channels or just accept that life doesn't always go the way we desire, other more passionate individuals (this is my polite way of saying 'absolute tossers') might go online and search for the email address of the comedian they despise in order to send them an honest and considered critique of their performance.

If you receive this sort of correspondence, the most important advice is **DO NOT REPLY**. The lunatics who send hate emails want to feel like they've got to you and it is far better to pretend you never even received the message in the first place or are simply too busy with showbusiness to respond. Remember: **DO NOT REPLY**.

As an example of the sort of email I am referring to, here is one I was lucky enough to receive after an appearance on Channel 4's *8 Out of 10 Cats*. It was sent to me at 3:02a.m. the morning after the episode had been transmitted by a gentleman called Brian . . .

From: *Brian Evans*
To: *Joe Lycett*
Subject: *8 out of 10 cars*

Just saw you on the show and had to email you to tell you: you are shit! Jimmy Carr is the best thing about that show by miles. Your not even remotely funny. heres some advice find another job!!! Your a dick!!!!
Brian Evans

███████████████████

Please consider the environment. Do you really need to print this email?

You will notice I've blocked out some text under Brian's name at the end of his email. The blocked-out text is his workplace address, a solicitors in Burnley. Remember, **DO NOT REPLY** to this sort of email.

Anyway, I replied. No one has ever left *their workplace address* on the bottom of their hate mail to me and I couldn't resist.

From: *Joe Lycett*
To: *Brian Evans*
Subject: *Re: 8 out of 10 cars*

Dearest Brian,
Thank you for your email regarding my recent appearance on '8 out of 10 cars', the spin-off show to the very popular '8 out of 10 cats'. I

welcome any and all feedback, and will endeavour to improve in the future. Can I ask, did you like my shirt? It was expensive!

I read with great interest your thoughts on Jimmy Carr. He is indeed a fantastic comedian and broadcaster. As you left the address of your workplace on your email signature, I have arranged for a signed photograph of Jimmy to be posted to you to thank you for your feedback.

Yours,

Joe Lycett

P.S. I will now spend some time considering the environment before printing your emails.

From: Brian Evans
To: Joe Lycett
Subject: Re: Re: 8 out of 10 cars

Please don't send me any stuff this is my work-place. Sorry about the last email I was drunk.

Brian

Despite Brian's impassioned plea I'd already sent him the following printout, which he would've had to sign for.

That's right, it's a picture of Jimmy Carr with my signature on it. Just a bit of fun. A few days later, as I am considerate, I sent a follow-up email.

From: *Joe Lycett*
To: *Brian Evans*
Subject: *Re: Re: Re: 8 out of 10 candles*

My beloved Brian,
Thank you for your apology but it is unnecessary – if anything, I actually owe you an apology as I've sent what is clearly my autograph on a Jimmy Carr picture! I practise my signature on leftover photographs of Jimmy and there must've been a clerical error.
I've had Jimmy's signature sent to you first class this morning, with my compliments.
Forever yours,
Joe Lycett

P.S. I am still considering the environment before printing your emails.

From: *Brian Evans*
To: *Joe Lycett*
Subject: *Re: Re: Re: Re: 8 out of 10 candles*

Please please don't send stuff to my office. Im sorry for sending the first email I was drunk.

Too late. I'd already sent him a Jimmy Carr autograph that I had taken from a Google search and added a penis to, simply because I like the idea of him opening it in the middle of a busy office.

(Jimmy has since informed me that, weirdly, this is exactly how he writes his signature.)

From: *Brian Evans*
To: *Joe Lycett*
Subject: *Re: Re: Re: Re: Re: 8 out of 10 candles*

Honestly mate what the actual fuck??? I've apologised and you're still sending stuff. This is my workplace man the glitter got everywhere. Please just FUCK OFF!!!!

Oh yes, I forgot to mention I put glitter in the envelope.
  Lots of it!

From: *Joe Lycett*
To: *Brian Evans*
Subject: *Re: Re: Re: Re: Re: Re: 8 out of 10 candles*

OK Brian, I'll stop sending you stuff.
  I should tell you I have finished my considerations as to the environment before printing your emails and have decided to print them regardless. They are in the post to your offices and addressed to 'the manager'.
Yours,
Joe Lycett

From: Brian Evans
To: Joe Lycett

Shit.

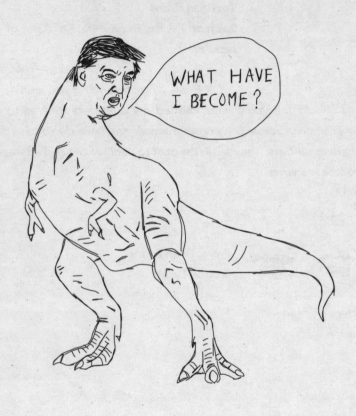

HOW TO
STOP DONALD TRUMP

When I first wrote this book this chapter was meant to be a light-hearted critique of a man who would never have a chance at power. Somehow he is now President. The way he behaves is so erratic and things change so rapidly that I can't guarantee that by the time this paperback edition goes to print he hasn't morphed in his dragon king form, or invaded the UK and banned all literature, or all books are obsolete because the earth is now a scorched rock with just one little island floating in the middle of the magma with a Trump Tower on it. Only you, dear reader of the future, truly know the horrors that follow these curious times.

For my part I continue to troll the brute and will endeavour to do so throughout his Presidency to the best of my ability. Of course I'm not going to actually go to America and actually protest in person or anything, I shan't be prised from my delicious bath, but I'll do it on Twitter. Immediately after the election I made a point of reminding him of his pledges:

@realDonaldTrump alright mate, quick q: what day will America be great again? Thinking of doing a trip next year, wanna book flights early!

Followed by this:

@realDonaldTrump Another quick one: when do you start on the wall? Dad's got a cement mixer in the garage, yours if you can collect.

At time of writing he has actually started on the wall – life has become a parody of itself. Perhaps I will meet a fox called Samantha Peterson next week? The cement mixer remains in the garage.

Beyond these initial offerings I've been using a pithier approach. I have made a point of responding every time Donald tweets something a bit stroppy (which is always) with just five letters: 'ok hun'. Hun is one of the finest, most under-rated words in the English language and a perfect way to refer to a President who gets his knickers in a twist over sizes of crowds or speeches by Meryl Streep.

Behold, some examples:

@realDonaldTrump
I cancelled today's meeting with the failing @nytimes when the terms and conditions of the meeting were changed at the last moment. Not nice.

reply from @joelycett
.@realDonaldTrump_ok hun

And this beaut:

@realDonaldTrump
Prior to the election it was well known that I have interests in property all over the world.Only the crooked media makes this a big deal!

reply from @joelycett
.@realDonaldTrump ok hun

My personal favourite was in response to this open goal, the week before his inauguration:

@realDonaldTrump
Intelligence agencies should never have allowed this fake news to "leak" into the public. One last shot at me.Are we living in Nazi Germany?

reply from @joelycett
.@realDonaldTrump not yet hun

These are dark and uncertain times and it is easy to lose hope amidst the lies and the sheer insanity. You could argue my approach is pointless, that he'll likely never see the tweets and even if he does he's the President of the USA and presumably too busy to be bothered. Bafflingly, all the evidence suggests this isn't true. Apparently Donald reads his tweets *regularly*, and they oft trigger bouts of fury and cause him immense stress, particularly when he feels he's being ridiculed. Those close to him allegedly try to shelter him from the jibes and the criticism. HE IS THE MOST POWERFUL MAN IN THE WORLD.

To see just how thin that satsuma skin really is, treat yourself to a browse of his Twitter feed immediately after any episode of American institution *Saturday Night Live*. If they've mocked him it can be reliably expected that he'll lash out, comment that the show is dreadful, that the impression of him is bad, and that it should be taken off air. HE IS THE MOST POWERFUL MAN IN THE WORLD.

This inability of power to cope with ridicule is one of the beautiful tools of comedy. Every comic knows that people like Trump, that cannot handle appearing as a fool, are a precious gift to their art. If only they knew their protests at being made to look a fool make them appear even more foolish! So if you want to get to him I urge you: join me. Make him look daft in whichever way you can. Tweet jokes at him, caricature him, make a sculpture of him with his knob out (I've done this) or just reply to him with 'ok hun'. What have you to lose?! It might be more effective than you think. And do it soon, because there's every chance he'll try and stop you in the future because he's Donald Trump and right now HE IS THE MOST POWERFUL MAN IN THE WORLD.

The key goals of my life are thus: spending a minimum of two hours a day in the bath, learning to dance to Bhangra music and stopping Donald Trump. I haven't the coordination to be a convincing dancer but I'll be happy if I manage two before I die.

I sometimes wonder if life would be dull without people like Donald Trump. Then I realise, no Joe, that's an absurd thing to think, life would just be far better. I'm not suggesting eradicating people like him entirely, merely gathering them all up and putting them somewhere that they can't do any more damage. Like in an active volcano, or the sea.

There are many things that trouble me about Donny Trumpyplops but the thing I find most worrying is his anti-Muslim rhetoric and his refusal to accept that the terrorists who commit heinous crimes 'in the name of Allah' are as rare and mentally challenged as the Westboro Baptist Church is to Christians.

There's also a crisis going on in Syria, where terrified civilians are fleeing in their millions. I think that countries like the US and the UK should be accepting these people, feeding them, homing them, including them, but people in power think that's a bad idea either 'cause it'll upset some people or because they're not sure if putting them all on a Megabus is technically worse for their human rights.

In 2015, a reporter from the reputable news source Fox News said that Birmingham was '100 per cent Muslim'. As a proud Brummie, I say to you: '*Salam alaikum.*' It was peculiar hearing that 'news', as I was in the Middle East at the time performing stand-up in Dubai, Abu Dhabi and Qatar. Friends of mine had warned me about travelling to these countries, claiming that 'they don't like,' as one friend put it, 'your lot.' I didn't know what he meant by my lot, presumably he was referring to fly fishers.

The punishment for homosexuality in these countries is oft jail, the logic of which I have never understood. 'Oh you like men? We'll put you in a box with some.' Not exactly a punishment, lads! I thought they stoned homosexuals to death out there but I've since discovered those deaths are merely because gays can't catch.

There's some truth to the claim that Birmingham is 100 per cent Muslim. There are a lot of Muslims, one of the most famous being Malala Yousafzai. Malala is brilliant – for those not familiar with her, she's a young schoolgirl who was shot by the Taliban for wanting to be educated and now goes to Edgbaston High School for Girls. It's a private school and it makes me livid to think she probably doesn't pay the fees. Personally, I'd hate to go to school with Malala Yousafzai. Show and Tell day would be a nightmare. I imagine the teacher saying to the class, 'Now, who's brought something in? Sally, let's start with you.' Sally meekly lifts her palm to reveal an ugly papier-mâché sculpture of a cat. 'OK class, anyone else? Malala?' Malala lifts up her Nobel Peace Prize. The teacher smiles. 'Sally. You're a piece of shit.'

Truth be told, I was annoyed when Fox News broadcast that Birmingham is 100 per cent Muslim and I'm annoyed with Donald Trump now, because saying somewhere is '100 per cent Muslim' or refusing to allow Muslims to enter a country perpetuates the myth that there is something terrifying about them. The problem, as I see it, is we are using the word 'Muslim' far too quickly to describe people committing terrorist atrocities, when they don't represent Muslims any more than I do.

My solution to this problem is simple: use a more accurate term for terrorists. I propose: 'Knobheads'. There would be levels of knobhead – you could have a 'moderate knobhead' all the way up to 'fundamental knobhead'. And if we all did it, the news would have to catch up. Imagine 6 o'clock bulletins with headlines like, 'TONIGHT: two knobheads have bombed a car' etc.

If you would like to read a thorough account of my approach to solving the problem of ISIS, it is documented later in this book and involves Grindr. Donald's solution is far more troubling and is essentially a blanket ban on Muslims entering the US, which inevitably stirs up more anger and is also probably really difficult to organise. I realised I had to try to stop him.

Trumpypumpy is a slippery fish. I have no delusions of grandeur – I understand that many of the finest minds in politics have struggled to hold him back and have failed, and that my influence and reach is minimal. So my approach was to do what I do best: be really bloody annoying.

I started with a good old-fashioned tweet. Trump tweeted a thinly veiled dig at Muslims:

@realDonaldTrump Wow, what a day. So many foolish people refuse to acknowledge the tremendous danger and uncertainty of certain people coming into the US.

I replied:

@joelycett .@realDonaldTrump new fone who dis?

He must've been too busy brushing his hair to reply. I thought over the problem for a long time (10–15 minutes) and soon realised a large part of his revenue stream comes from his hotels. Damaging *them* damages *him*. I decided to review them online.

Let me explain: the ability for anyone to give their opinion on literally anything these days is something that concerns me deeply, but that doesn't stop me absolutely loving review websites. They effectively allow every jobless loser with half an idea to tell entrepreneurs who have been running successful businesses for years – sometimes for generations – how to improve the recipe of their tuna sandwich. It must make them absolutely livid when they read that Great-grandma's recipe for fish stew 'is watery and tasteless'. Yeah, sure Great-grandma, you've been dead for fifty years, but just so you know, your stew tastes like shit.

I decided to spend some time writing reviews of Trump's hotels in the hope that it might begin to damage his business and inadvertently weaken his campaign. Many would've taken the obvious route of just slagging the residences off, saying the beds were uncomfortable and there were rats in the restaurant, but I decided a more subtle and arguably idiotic approach would be preferable.

Here are a few examples:

TRUMP INTERNATIONAL GOLF LINKS & HOTEL IRELAND

Fantastic hotel. I came to play golf and stayed for the leisure facilities! I must say, the golf course was really fantastic – as good as any I've been to, and I've been to three. The rooms were spacious and warm. I was also pleased to see that when a family of Muslims came in, they were tasered to the ground and removed. Couldn't ask for more. FIVE STARS.

👍 👍 👍 👍 👍

TRUMP INTERNATIONAL HOTEL & TOWER NEW YORK

Ordered room service pizza and the toppings were a disgrace, the cheese almost non-existent. Make America Great Again?! More like Make America GRATE Again!! Breakfast was pretty good though, two types of sausage. TWO STARS

👍 👍

TRUMP INTERNATIONAL HOTEL & TOWER CHICAGO

A really relaxing stay, very comfortable and some lovely pictures of Donald Trump were on display on the walls. It is such a testament to him that he has achieved so much and gained so many votes when he looks like a Lego head that has been put into a microwave. FOUR STARS.

👍 👍 👍 👍

I was very proud of these and thus hugely disappointed when the website I was using refused to publish them. I suppose I probably shouldn't have claimed I was staying in Ireland, New York and Chicago at the same time. You live, you learn.

Despairing, I went back to the drawing board. How else could I disrupt his businesses? I realised his policies are anti-refugee and anti-Muslim; he's frightened of them, and so are many of his supporters.

So I tried to book Syrian refugees into his hotels. I contacted as many managers of Trump Hotels as I could find an email for, asking on behalf of a 'big group'. How's at least a million for you? Most of them spotted me coming a mile off (maybe they thought 'Samantha Salamander' sounded like a Muslim name?), but I did get close with one establishment.

After a little back and forth, the manager of one of them sent me some charming pictures of the rooms – a little like this:

Plenty of room for Syrian refugees! Enthusiastically, I responded.

These look fantastic!

What is the capacity of those rooms do you think? Looking at the photographs I reckon I could get three people on the bed, then maybe another two on the floor around the bed, then about 6 people in the living area. It'll be cosy but it'll work!

So if we say 11 people per room, across 27 rooms, that's space for 297?

Many thanks,

Paul

I thought this was a measured response, but it was clear from their reply I had pushed them too far.

Mr Paulington,

In New York we have very strict safety restrictions and fire regulations – 2 persons per bedroom or 4 persons per suite, and most hotels in the city adhere to a similar policy. Although I feel we are not the best partner hotel for your upcoming group, I wish you the very best of luck with your search.

Hotel Manager

I tried, valiantly, to respond to this.

That's absolutely fine – we only intend to have two fires per room. We can have one for cooking and one for keeping everyone warm. If regulations only allow one, then we can work round that.

I know we have a few issues to iron out with regulations and so on but I've told the refugees to make their way to your address and we can cross those bridges when we come to them. There's about half a million of them on their way.

Many thanks,

Paul

Alas, contact stopped from this point on. Even this completely foolproof tactic had failed.

My political influence was used elsewhere in the Republican campaign though, as I credit myself with one of the key candidates, Jeb Bush, removing himself from the race. Again, the power of Twitter was key. Republican candidates up against Trump had begun to engage in more and more desperate activities in an attempt to claw back some of the votes they'd lost to the blond bombshell. Jeb Bush decided he was losing votes because he hadn't made it clear enough to gun-loving voters just how much he also loved guns. To rectify the matter, he posted one of the weirdest things I've ever seen a politician, or anyone, put on Twitter. The tweet was merely a picture of a gun with his name engraved on it, and the caption 'America'.

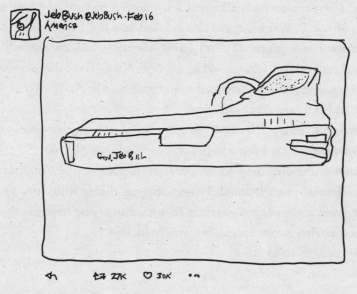

In many ways, this was an open goal for me and my reply was simple.

Yes, I responded with a British insitution, a picture of a simple cup of tea. I expect it was English Breakfast but I don't want to speculate too much. To my great surprise and considerable delight, my tweet was picked up by BBC News and other serious news outlets, despite it being a stupid joke on a social networking site and thus arguably not 'news'.

A week later, Jeb Bush pulled out of the race. Some say coincidence, I say I am a key player in American politics.

Unfortunately, despite my clear influence in the American Presidential race, Donald Trump slipped through my net and remained a key player. Essentially, what I'm trying to say is this: if you're American, I tried, but you're fucked.

HOW TO
DEAL WITH
NOSY NEIGHBOURS

When I am on the road performing my jaw-achingly hilarious stand-up, I prefer to stay with friends rather than in hotels where possible because I can check out whenever I want and don't have to pay an extra fee when I inevitably shit the bed.

I was doing a run of shows in the South West and stayed with a dear friend who I am calling Sheila to protect her privacy. Sheila is one of life's good eggs – you could conservatively describe her as 'eclectic' or if you were being a little more liberal you might say she is 'absolutely bat-shit-off-her-nut crazy'. Either way, I think she's the best.

Sheila has lived in her house for some time, which is a mixture of colourful mismatched blankets, flowers and ashtrays. She's a true creative and a single woman, owning somewhere in the region of 10 million cats. She's fairly relaxed about clothing, her meals consist of the stuff that's in her fridge (yoghurt, couscous, orange and Quorn mince was one culinary masterpiece she produced for me) and she loves loud classical music.

The tenants next door were about to move out escaping just after a year of being Sheila's neighbour. She said the husband, Simon, seemed alright but the wife, Linda, was a bit of a prude and had complained about some things over the twelve months. She said, 'She sends me emails warning me there are leaves in the gutter.' What a bore.

As a farewell, Linda had sent Sheila a parting email. Knowing I was arriving soon and had expertise in this area, she decided to delay replying until I had been consulted. The email she received is one of my favourites, a mixture of awkwardness, passive aggression and plain old-fashioned neighbourly complaint.

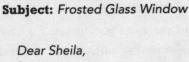

Subject: *Frosted Glass Window*

Dear Sheila,

As you know, Simon and I are moving next month and we wanted to say how nice it has been living next to you. However, I did want to mention something before we left. I had been trying to find a way of avoiding emailing about it, as I was terribly embarrassed, but I think you should be aware for the new tenants.

There is a window to the side of the house with frosted glass that I presume to be part of your bathroom. When anyone stands near the frosted glass without the blind down, you might be shocked to hear it basically covers nothing! It is particularly bad at night. Simon alerted me to it a few months ago and I was terribly shocked when I first saw. We try to avert our eyes but, as you can understand, sometimes it is impossible.

I am sorry it has taken me so long to send this but I have been terribly embarrassed by the whole thing. I'm sure it can be resolved with a thicker blind?

I'm sure I'll see you before we leave, best of luck with everything.
Best,
Linda

What a treat of an email and sent at 10a.m. on a Sunday morning! What a time to send news that you have been involved in an accidental strip show in your own house! I enquired as to why Linda was informing her now, forcing Sheila to reveal 'The night before it was sent I had a bath and then did some plucking near that window.' I did not enquire for further specifics as I was trying to enjoy my meal of veggie sausages, sliced cucumber and fruit compote.

Sheila is not the sort of person who has care for clothing and would happily be naked at all times. Her clothes are always loose fitting, as if she has just thrown a sheet over herself, but she is constantly ready to whip them off and get skin to the wind. I can imagine that the display at that window was, at times, akin to a hardcore low-budget sex cam. I bet Simon, Linda's husband, had a fabulous time.

It must be stressed that the window itself is not easily viewed from Linda's house. Linda (or, let's be realistic, Simon) would basically need to be outside next to her garage to get any substantial view of Sheila's plucking session. Why either of them would be hanging around outside their garage at night is a mystery.

I asked Sheila how daft she wanted to be about this and she said, 'FULL DAFT'. We drafted and sent the following in the early afternoon.

Subject: *Frosted Glass Window – Explanation*

Hello Linda!

Thank you for your email. I have been waiting for this email for some time and I'm glad you finally found the courage.

The truth is I had deliberately left the blind up because, I am not ashamed to say, I have been trying to seduce you. I have been on this road for a number of years and have met many different tenants of your current house. There have been a small handful whom I have found irresistible. You are one of them.

When this happens I devise a sexual dance, which I do in the frosted window, at key times throughout the day, to attract and allure. I know that it is somewhat difficult to get a good look at that window from your property and so I now know the arousal was reciprocated, because you would have to have made the effort to go out next to the garage and watch.

I'm glad you've finally got in touch just before you leave. I will endeavour to increase the frequency of my dances for the remainder of your tenancy.

Best,

Sheila

x

We opened a bottle of Prosecco at this point to celebrate our silliness. I expected Linda would ponder her reply for a few days, but within twenty minutes a message popped up in Sheila's inbox.

Subject: *Re: Frosted Glass Problem – Explanation*

Bit confused by that email. Is this a joke? I'm happily married to Simon.
Best,
Linda

Sorry Linda, there has been some confusion. It wasn't you I was trying to seduce, but Simon. Could you pass this on to him? And thank him for being a loyal audience to my seductive window ballets.
Sheila

I must say I wasn't expecting, and really admire, the next reply. Simon clearly saw what was going on, that we were at FULL DAFT, and came back DOUBLE FULL DAFT.

Sheila,
Simon here. Linda has shown me your emails! I'm flattered but happily married. I do have some tips for the future:

- Maybe invest in some back lighting, to create a silhouette, as the current lighting can be unflattering and confusing, meaning I sometimes had to zoom my binoculars in to fully comprehend what was going on.

- Whilst I enjoyed most of the performances, some of them were what I would describe as 'experimental'. If you want to captivate your audience, you may want to encourage their trust with some more traditional performances, instead of launching straight into 'naked teeth flossing'.

- Perhaps wear a little more clothing at the start of your dances. Leave something to the imagination, at least at the beginning!

   - Have you thought about back-up dancers? They can really take the heat off when you're not at the top of your game.

   I hope you take my comments on board for future suitors. I think you've got a raw talent that could really be refined to something spectacular.

Many thanks,

Simon (and Linda)

Simon (and Linda),
How rude. I'll be glad to see the back of you.
Sheila

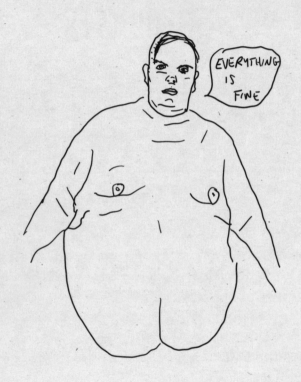

HOW TO STOP ISIS

ISIS, or SO-CALLED ISIS, or ISIL, or IS, or Daesh, or IS-Fernandez-Versini – whatever you want to call them, they are BAD. EGGS. They behead people, destroy historic landmarks and throw gay men off buildings. Which now I think about it doesn't sound that different to a few stag dos I've heard about. Am I right lads?! I'm not wrong!

Recently, I have read a few reports of people and businesses called Isis that have had real problems since the terrorist group popularised the name. I've often wondered what happens to those who have a name that becomes sullied. I bet there were still a ton of guys called Adolf in Germany post-1945, and I bet people in the Garden of Eden called Adam and Eve were livid after that snake situation. The worst I've encountered is a cement-mixing company based in Smethwick called 'Jim'll Mix It', who I imagine must really be regretting that beautiful pun work now.

And so to Isis Taylor, a porno actress based in San Francisco. I found her after a Twitter search for the terrorist group, as I was looking for photographs of their members for a little project I had going on. More on that later. She appears to be pretty popular and, according to my friend who did some proper research on her, 'very good at what she does'. I'll leave you to research that in your own time.

Unfortunately for Isis, I noticed she had posted her email address on one of her tweets, so I got long-time porn fan Paul Paulington to get in touch.

From: PAUL PAULINGTON
To: Isis Taylor
Subject: Shocked

Dear Isis,

I have been a loyal and devoted fan of your work as an actress for a number of years now and have long thought you are a beautiful and talented performer.

However, my opinion of you was changed after I read a recent newspaper article about you. I am SHOCKED and CONCERNED, Isis, to learn that you have taken over swathes of Iraq and eastern Syria and intend to create an Islamic caliphate in the region.

I implore you to see sense and return to your porn career in San Francisco.

Yours with concern,

Paul Paulington

P.S. Please can I request a signed copy of Round Mound of Ass 6.

Isis did reply, explaining – quite rightly – that Paul Paulington is a fucking idiot.

Back to the terrorist group. I have been trying for some time now to decipher why someone would join ISIS. I can't see the appeal myself – it seems pretty full-on, plus they don't seem to have a reliable source of halloumi. In other words, it is basically hell on earth. My fascination arose after reading an article about an ISIS militant from the UK who had moved to Syria and was, bizarrely, writing a blog about his experiences. He was disappointed with the distinct lack of manners his compatriots had and complained that people would steal his phone charger and every time he went to pray someone would nab his shoes. OMG SO TRUE. I've lost count of the number of times I've dismantled my entire life in the Western world, moved to Syria, joined a barbaric extremist group and only then found that they don't share the same respect for footwear as me. It's one of my number-one gripes.

Part of me quite likes the idea that every time ISIS release a video threatening the West, that particular militant is looking really closely at the guy's shoes in the footage and one day will shout at the screen, 'He's wearing my bloody pumps!'

After much thought, I realised that people join ISIS because they suffer from a lack of love. Over time, a lack of love can wear away at your soul, creating a cyclical mix of self-loathing and hatred of the world, ending in violence and barbarism. You can't throw a gay off a building with love in your heart – believe me, I've tried! Sorry, Carlos!

It's all the more sad that love is lacking when some of them are SUPER cute. Sure, they're an acquired taste, but if you have a penchant for bearded men with a sassy attitude, look no further.

ISIS are a massive organisation with branches all over the world – I am but one, admittedly big-hearted, man but my love will not be enough. I am prepared to show them love, but I wanted to see if there was love elsewhere in the world for ISIS militants. So I went to the place where love flows like water. Grindr.

I scoured the image results from an Internet search for 'sexy terrorist' and uploaded the most alluring onto the popular gay dating app Grindr, in the hope that someone would want to meet up with them. Then they would know at least in some small way that there are people out there willing to love them, and the appeal of a shoeless life in Syria would be diminished.

To those who aren't familiar, Grindr is a gay dating app. And I'm stretching the definition of the word 'dating' a lot. It's an absolute shag fest. The first was with Craig . . .

CRAIG

Lol are you Isis?

Yes. Death to the West.

Omg I know a drag act called Alexandra Burka You'd love her

What is she?

She sings show tunes in a burka. That's it really.

> Doesn't sound very good

> Yeh to be fair it is shit.
> Wanna meet?

SUCCESS! Craig is up for meeting an ISIS militant. Another one saved from a trip to Syria!

The second conversation was with a guy called James.

JAMES

> Wanna blow?

> What building?

[I was pleased with that.]

> Okayyyy

> Tell me more about yourself.

> I serve the Islamic state.
> You?

> i serve in wagamamas.

> Tell me. If you could do anything what would you want to do to me?

> I would destroy you and your civilisation

> thats hot. Where shall we meet?

In hell.

Is that a nightclub?

It is always night time in hell

Weird. Gotta go.

Another success! There were people falling over themselves to date an ISIS guy.

And that wasn't all – Edward got in touch . . .

EDWARD

Hello handsome! What's your name?

I have no name. I serve islamic state in Syria.

Syria?

Yes. I'm syrious.

It says you're 1.4 miles away.

I'm in a sleeper cell.

Wanna sleep in my cell?

No.

Wat u doing in the pic?

Cleaning my AK47.

Cool. What u gonna do with it?

I will use it to destroy the West.

Wanna destroy my asshole first?

Play it cool, Ed. I find the the phrase 'destroy my asshole' is best reserved until the third date. Despite that, I'm claiming that as a success!

The fourth and final convo is with a guy called Barry:

BARRY

a/s/l

18/m/syria

syria??

yes. dath to the west.

death*

haha

well we probably can't meet cause im in milton keynes

milton keynes is full of whores who are all going to hell

omg tell me about it!!

I'm going to argue that wasn't unsuccessful either – I'm fairly sure Barry would've agreed to meet if there wasn't the slight geography issue.

It's clear, there is more than enough love to go around.

So to those thinking of joining ISIS, I say: Don't. Join Grindr.

THEY SAY WE NEED MORE
BOOTS ON THE GROUND
IN SYRIA

BUT I CAN'T SEE HOW A
PHARMACY AND SAME DAY
PHOTO PRINTING CAN HELP.

HOW TO
BUY THE PERFECT GIFT

One of the most consistently stressful and difficult tasks in an adult's life is buying a gift. Many people ask me, 'Joe, it's my friend/loved one/relative/boss/prostitute's birthday next Tuesday. What should I buy them?' I look them dead in the eye and say, 'How did you get into my dressing room? I have a taser.'

I was once tasked with buying a retirement present for an employee at an office I was temping at. Debbie was leaving after twenty-four years of tedium, but the manager was too busy to go out for an hour and get a gift himself. Instead he felt it appropriate to send a teenager who had been making bad cups of tea for three weeks and who couldn't buy a coat that fit him properly out on this important mission. I had a budget of £50 and twenty-four hours. After some considerations (exactly three thoughts) and some serious panicking, I got her a £20 gift voucher for Next, a £20 voucher for HMV and a box of £7.99 Classic Collection Thornton chocolates. I pocketed the other £2.01 and I have no regrets. Debbie cried, which I take as a victory. She's probably dead now, so what does it matter? I expect she was buried wearing a lovely Next dress.

When you gift someone something you give them not only the gift itself but the awkwardness of trying to pretend they love it more than their own family when it is a pen. And that is one of the single most important things I have discovered about gift-giving – it is predominantly about making the other person feel awkward and bad. There is nothing worse than the crippling guilt of receiving a Christmas present from someone you haven't got anything for. Thus, if someone has avoided my WhatsApp messages for a few days I like to surprise them with a small but lavish offering, something thoughtful, something to be cherished. It'll be a really fantastic, sarcastically expensive present, with a gushing note about how they really helped me through some particularly hard times.

I discovered this useful form of punishment in my early years at university. There was a group of thin, sexually alluring girls who would congregate together and clumsily bitch about literally anyone and everyone. They would've bitched about an unborn baby. I loved it. I wanted to be in their gang.

There was a spanner in the works, however, as I was not a cool, athletic stud of a boy but a rotund and spotty wimp draped in dreary cardigans. Despite a certain flair and charm, they never wanted me in their core group. This is perfectly understandable as I would've brought the mean weight up too significantly and that would be terrible PR. Naturally they kept me at arm's length using their main weapon: bitching. I was allowed to indulge in their company for a short while but it would not last long and, much like cats, once I got too close they would lash out, walk to the other side of the room and lick their vaginas. Manchester University was a wonderful place.

During the brief time they let me breathe the same air, I learnt that Becky, who was arguably the worst of the group, had a great love of horses and in fact owned a couple back home in Hurtful Commentshire or wherever it was that she lived. She would talk a lot about horses and had an enviable armoury of horse-themed stationery, if you can find horse-themed stationery enviable, which you can't. I once made a joke about 'feeling a little horse' and she didn't laugh. God, she was a twat.

Anyway, one afternoon I was looking around an old vintage shop and discovered a beautiful horse pin. It was a delightful depiction of a galloping horse, delicately crafted out of brass and about the size of a two-pence piece. It was only £4, so I bought it and gave it to her. She was so shocked by this act of unsolicited kindness, from someone whom she had been so consistently vile to, that she couldn't cope and I watched as her face imploded with guilt. It was as if every barbed comment, every disgusted look she had made at me had immediately reversed direction and spun directly at her withered soul, fuelled by spiteful kindness.

Since we've left university, Becky has become a single mother and I don't hear much from her, other than online every hour of every day when she posts old clips from *Top Gear* or complains about benefit cheats to Facebook. She asked for free tickets to one of my shows once. GOOD LUCK, MATE.

I have used this technique more knowingly since. I believe it is referred to colloquially as 'killing with kindness' but I prefer 'torturing with treats'. This is because there is no 'killing', no sweet release from the guilt, but a lifetime of occasionally remembering how you once laughed at Leanne for wearing a dress from New Look and she looked really hurt by it, and then she got you in the Secret Santa and gave you what is now your favourite belt. Sorry, but Leanne wins.

So, if you make a misjudged comment about my outfit on a night out: expect to receive a beautiful Pandora bracelet with a passive-aggressive 'Elephants Never Forget' charm. Consistently ignore my texts? You'll soon be accepting a Fortnum & Mason hamper with a hand-painted Christmas card. Don't congratulate me on my new hair? Expect some anthrax.

In terms of gift-buying for someone you actually like – have you thought about buying them this book? I won't stop you. Otherwise, maybe try something like flowers or a nice bit of jewellery? Oh I don't know, they're not my mate. What do you think this is, a self-help book?

Piss off.

I HATE TRYING TO FIND GIFTS
FOR PEOPLE I DON'T LIKE.
PLUS, IT'S A NIGHTMARE
TRYING TO WRAP CAT SHIT.

HOW TO RESPOND TO HOMOPHOBIA

There's one sure-fire way to get under my skin and that's being homophobic. I suppose it's because it throws me back to complex and frustrating emotions I had as a child but also it is so boring. Come on, guys! We don't hate gays any more, we hate Muslims!

It was around my thirteenth birthday when I first noticed other children calling me, or rather *accusing* me of being gay. I had no idea what I was (I still don't in many ways), but my response was to develop my first heckle put-down. I would simply say, 'Don't bend over then!' That was quite the curveball from a 13-year-old and created such confusion that whoever was picking on me would generally just leave me alone. Just so we're clear, yes, I wrote an anal rape gag when I was thirteen.

Though it seemed to be more present and acceptable when I was a boy, thankfully casual homophobia appears less these days. Back then everyone seemed to be doing it, not just the students – even one of my PE teachers told me after a game of rugby to 'leave your handbag at home next time'. I was disgusted. It was clearly a clutch.

In some ways I now find it quite funny in its absurdity. I'm just sort of baffled that after all this time folks are STILL trying to argue that there's something wrong with it, that it is in some way indulgent, that it is the devil's work. Whilst I notice homophobia less and less, what I do notice has diversified. It's not just chubby middle-aged ale-soaked men down the pub any more, even gay people themselves engage in it. Dolce & Gabbana recently said that gay couples adopting a child is 'unnatural'. Biphobia is a thing now – Christopher Biggins took a pop by saying in an interview that bisexual men 'ruin women's lives'. I once saw Biggins in panto and it ruined all of our afternoons, male and female. Nah, I'm only joking. He's very talented.

My local MP is a man called Roger Godsiff, who has a safe seat and weird eyebrows. It was brought to my attention that he was going to vote against gay marriage the weekend after I'd just been to the most fabulous gay civil partnership. It was so much more fun than any straight wedding even though everyone there will go to hell as punishment. I sort of cringe at this letter when I read it back cause it's a little earnest and preachy. But I'm glad I sent it.

Dear Roger,

I am one of your constituents and it has been brought to my attention that you are voting against gay marriage today. I find this disappointing.

Denying gay people the opportunity to marry, instead referring to it as a 'civil partnership', legitimises considering gay people as others and not full and equal members of society. The gay community has suffered greatly already as a result of archaic perceptions; voting against equal marriage continues this unnecessarily and is damaging for everyone. Furthermore, as a Labour MP you are also voting against your party line, which is 'equality for all'.

I believe a day will come when gay marriage will be legal and celebrated, if not in this vote then in a future one. In the future gay marriage will be so unremarkable as to not deserve comment. Children will come out and take for granted that they too can live a full and happy life and not fear that they are somehow different or incomplete. In that future it will be up to parents to remind their children, 'There wasn't always gay marriage.' They'll have to explain, 'A long time ago, gay people were considered not to be proper people and so couldn't express their love for one another like everyone else.' And those children will think, 'How stupid! How short-sighted of those silly people in the past!'

Don't be that silly person, Roger.

Regards,

Joe Lycett

P.S. Empty my pigging bins.

He didn't reply, but he also abstained from voting.

One recent homophobe to emerge is World Heavyweight Champion Tyson Fury, who claims that homosexuality is evil and unnatural, whereas his job is the most natural thing in the world: punching people in the head.

I get the appeal of boxing. You get to wear fun shorts and look really tough and cool. I bet some women respond to the testosterone of it and you end up feeling really attractive and masculine. BUT IT IS A VERY GAY SPORT. Two topless sweaty men touching each other's faces. That's gay. So it's a bit rich that Tyson, Heavyweight Champion and thus King of the Gays, has compared homosexuality to paedophilia. Oh and abortion. All very similar things, I think you'll agree.

Whilst I personally find it annoying and boring, it's clear that there are many advocates coming out and announcing: 'Mum! Dad! I'm homophobic!' I'm a great believer in bringing people together – rather than call people names or accuse them of being stupid it is far better to engage with them, ask them why they think the things they do and offer alternative viewpoints. Just because we disagree and you think because I'm not straight I'm going to hell, doesn't mean we can't be friends!

It got me thinking: there must be some way we can merge homosexuality AND homophobia into a spectacular event. With the gayest homophobe I know front and centre: Tyson Fury.

The best place to find gays, other than on Old Compton Street or Simon Cowell's phone book, is the theatre. But homophobes generally hate the theatre. It's even worse if it's gay theatre. Which is basically all theatre. So I devised a show that would change all that and pitched it, in the guise of my alter ego Peter Peterson, to Tyson's agent Sue. Please note my opening line, which I am more proud of than anything I have ever achieved previously.

To: *Sue*
From: *Peter Peterson*
Subject: *TYSON FURY: Availability Check*

To Sue It May Concern,

I'm contacting you regarding an exciting opportunity for your client Tyson Fury. I am producing a one-off West End Theatre Spectacular entitled 'TYSON FURY & THE SEVEN GAY DWARFS'. This will be the first show to deliberately appeal to homosexuals and homophobes alike and naturally we would love Tyson to be the epicentre.

The premise of the play is simple. Tyson wakes up in a mystery cabin surrounded by dwarfs. At first he quite enjoys their company, as they feed him grapes and kumquats (budget allowing). But just before the interval it is revealed the cabin is a Soho nightclub and the dwarfs are GAY!! In the second act, Tyson chases them around the auditorium, screaming his catchphrase, 'I will kill you dead, dwarf' and knocking each one out, as our live band performs a scat-jazz version of Adele's 'Hello'. In the thrilling finale, we see Tyson tear off his shirt and shout, 'SEE YOU IN HELL, GAY DWARFS!'

Other songs in the production will include a cover of 'All That Jazz' retitled to 'All That Jizz' and a gay cover of 'Come On Eileen', changed to 'Come on David'. We will also be serving a selection of Gay foods in the interval, including Lemon Jizzle Cake and Corn on the Knob.

We are close to securing a West End theatre and tickets go on sale next week. I have designed a flyer (attached) and we are printing 100,000 copies today, to be given out with the **Evening Standard**. I have drawn smiley faces for the dwarfs as they are not yet confirmed. Tyson's fee will be equity minimum.

Please could you let me know if he can't do it for any reason ASAP.
Kind Regards,
Peter Peterson

Producer
Peter Peterson Productions

HOW TO
CLAIM PPI

If you're a human being, then you may have heard of a thing called PPI. I'm not really sure what it is and I'm not about to find out now, but I think it is either some sort of bacterial infection of the urethra or an illegal insurance policy that some financial institutions offered up years back, thinking they'd get away with it. Either way, it's a real pain in the dick.

Since then, some judge somewhere has quite rightly said that the banks did indeed behave irresponsibly (which is so unlike them!) and they all have to hand the money back to anyone who makes a valid claim. Loads of people have already and it's really pissed the banks off and I love it.

But as my great-grandmother always said, 'Where there's money, there's a dickhead', and a whole slew of companies have popped up to exploit this new revenue stream. They claim to specialise in helping you win back thousands of pounds, ignoring the fact you can do it easily on your own without involving anyone else at all and for free. They'll take about a 30 per cent commission, which is kind of like every time I gift someone a bottle of wine and then demand they open it immediately and pour me a glass.

Like any respectable company, these PPI experts oft canvass for business by texting mobile numbers at random with poorly written promises that they'll secure you loads of money. And, perhaps surprisingly, some of these companies are run by idiots.

For a while, there was one particular number that would text me about three times a week. The message that annoyed me the most came through just before I was about to go on stage. It read:

> Do you have PPI??? Did you know you could claim back £thousands? For more information text back YES. To stop receiving these messages text back STOP.

What sort of prick writes 'thousands of pounds' as '£thousands'? And THREE question marks??? Get in the bin, mate. I went on stage livid. I finished my show and replied immediately, full of adrenaline:

> Piss off love

Unbelievably, this didn't work!
The following day, another text.

> There are £thousands of pounds (£££) waiting for you in unclimaed PPI!!! Text back YES for more info. Text STOP to cancel

Well who would've thought it, I have thousands of pounds that have gone UNCLIMAED. I took this as a declaration of war, which was perhaps an overreaction. The real danger lay in the fact that I was now at home and I was bored. And this is a bad combination.

A really good trick if you're being spammed with texts or calls is to put the number that is bothering you into Google. There are a number of websites these days where people with nothing better to do post about the nuisance texts and calls they've received, explaining in great detail what happened to them, what they said back, what they were wearing when it happened and what medication they're on. Despite thinking these people are the key prizewinners of Loser of the Year, I still find their posts useful in determining who is ringing me.

For this particular number a Google search threw up a few posts:

'Just a chancer, just a guy texting from his personal number'
'NOT A PROPER COMPANY! The guy didnt know what he was on about!!!! AVOID!!!'
'PPI number, just spam not worth it'
'PPI or something. guy seemed alright, nice tone of voice'

Despite being reassured that he had a 'nice tone of voice', I've never taken out PPI insurance so he was wasting both my time and his own. And this was war. I decided to dive down the PPI rabbit hole:

YES

Thank you for replying. This is Martin. Can I ask which bank you took the insurance with.

YES

Just hearing the name gave me his whole life history. Something about the name Martin made me a bit sad. I don't know what it is, maybe it makes me think of Martin Clunes. Or suggests to me an individual who is just plodding along, not meaning any harm but ultimately getting in the way. Martin grew up in a small city and struggled with learning difficulties at school. He has well-meaning but ultimately uninterested friends who have probably got a fair bit further in life than Martin and he feels inadequate alongside them. Most of the people he knew growing up moved to London and are now bankers and lawyers, the friends who stayed local never really ask him what he's up to and secretly wish they didn't have to invite him to their after-work drinks. He tries to dress like he's really cool but he just gets it slightly wrong and ends up looking like he's trying too hard.

But Martin has dreams of grandeur. He's going to break out of the shackles society has incarcerated him in. He'll prove he's worth something, worth more than the rest of them. He'll show the whole world when he's a successful multimillionaire businessman. He's just got the small question of how to make his fortune? He hasn't the skills, or the ideas, or the patience.

He'll try texting me about my PPI.

And that makes him a twat.

Which bank did you take the insurance with?

BARCLAYS

Thank you. Can you estimate how much you are owed?

£THOUSANDS

Do you have any documents you can send me?

YES

Please send the documents.

Not sure that's the right picture. Are you sure it sent right?

NO

OK have you got any more?
I think there's perhaps something wrong with your phone. When did you take out the loan?

15 YEARS AGO.

I don't think I can help you I'm afraid, you can only claim for the last 10 years. Thank you.

YOU HAVE FAILED ME, MARTIN.

I left the matter to one side for a while as I was busy experimenting to see if olive oil is relaxing to bathe in. I can confirm it is, but getting out of the tub is farcical and incredibly dangerous.

Some three weeks later I stumbled across an app that promised to send automated text messages from my phone as often as I wished. Last time I got a phone contract I treated myself to unlimited text messages and so I figured now was the ideal time to test just how far 'unlimited' would stretch. Turns out unlimited does mean unlimited. Fabulous.

I put Martin's number into the app and scheduled it to send the message 'YOU HAVE FAILED ME, MARTIN' every thirty minutes, forever. This was merciful, I could've programmed it to send every five minutes.

The first five messages or so were ignored. Then, clearly beginning to find it irksome, Martin replied.

> OK I get it. Could you stop sending me these messages please?

> NO. YOU HAVE FAILED ME, MARTIN

After another day or so of sending the same message, I got a further reply from a now despairing Martin.

> OK not funny any more please stop these.

> YOU FORGET SO QUICKLY
> YOU HAVE FAILED ME, MARTIN

> YOU HAVE FAILED ME, MARTIN

I kept the app sending the messages. Martin stopped replying. After a week, the messages stopped being delivered. He'd clearly either blocked my number or changed his. This war was won.

I'll never know Martin's new number, I'll never know the true Martin. I hope he makes his fortune someday, I really do.

But if you're reading this Martin, never forget.

YOU HAVE FAILED ME, MARTIN.

NAN CALMLY CHANGED HER HAIR COLOUR
WHILST TAKING A NAP.

SHE DYED PEACEFULLY
IN HER SLEEP.

HOW TO
SURVIVE IN THE WILD

Bear Grylls is a man who goes to fields and forests and tries to live in them even though we have perfectly nice houses that provide warmth and have working apparatus for cooking food. Because of course, whilst you and I think living with heating, double glazing, refrigeration, and modern toilets is a reasonable way to live, Bear thinks it is WEAK and PATHETIC. Look at you shitting in a toilet bowl. Could you shit on a ski slope? Of course you couldn't. Bear can. I actually did once, but not voluntarily. It was a long way back down, I can tell you.

One day not long ago I went for a nice lunch with some friends in London and one of my pals had invited some bore called Damion who enjoyed telling us how 'no one has the skills to survive in the wild any more' and 'we're too reliant on manufactured human products'. Well excuse me for enjoying this delicious quinoa and goat's cheese salad in a comfortable and relaxed restaurant: let me take my clothes off, go out into the street, carve a crude spear from a twig and hunt for my lunch around Central London instead. 'What did I have for lunch today, you ask? Half a pigeon, which I captured with my fists. I only ate half 'cause most of it tasted like batteries.'

It's because of people like Damion that we can't enjoy modern life without feeling weak or guilty that we are somehow damaging the environment. Damion wants us all to be hunter-gatherers because he thinks that'll make him happy, even though the reason he's unhappy is because his acting career hasn't progressed beyond non-speaking roles in soap operas and he's in debt with his old drama school. Sorry, Damion, but if we were all hunter-gatherers we'd all die out pretty quickly. You need masses of wild open land to sustain even a small group of people who are hunting, it's an inefficient and archaic way of sourcing food, and it's cold. So stop trying to make me feel guilty 'cause I haven't foraged for all the ingredients in this quiche and spend more time learning your lines before an audition.

I don't mind Bear because he's not sanctimonious about it – he doesn't necessarily want us all to leave our houses and jobs (then there'd be no one at home in front of the television to watch his programmes!), but he wants the power of knowing that if modern society fell to shit, he would be our king. King Bear. Sounds like a dreadful indie band.

However, Bear hasn't got all the answers. I have compiled some of my own approaches to living the wild life. Whereas Bear will provide tips like 'drink your own urine if you get thirsty' or 'scavenge for nuts and berries', I have some more unusual but no less helpful tips to help you if you decide you want to live in a bush like a complete and utter fucking loser loner.

BUILD YOURSELF A NEST LIKE A BIRD

Birds are incredibly resourceful, collecting twigs and moss to create a super-comfy and chic pad to raise their youngsters in. And now, you can too! Grab loads of sticks and make a sort of bowl shape, add leaves and other soft things like flower petals to the inside, and curl up in the middle. Create a blanket out of your own hair. Die alone.

TWEET LIKE A BIRD

No I don't mean tweeting like on the Internet silly, I mean make the noise that other birds make in the hope that they respond. Someone somewhere has discovered that birds actually form structured sentences with syntax with commands like 'come over here' and 'bring food'. If you perfect your bird-speak you could have them do your bidding. Perhaps one day you will be able to talk to them on such a deep level that they would understand you. Although you struggle speaking to humans without them dying of boredom, so I doubt you're going to be much more impressive to a chaffinch.

COLLECT YOUR TEARS

You'll probably find that you cry a lot when thinking about the perfectly reasonable and acceptable life you left behind in this vain attempt to look like you're more manly and resourceful than everyone else. Every time this happens, put a small vial under your eyes to collect the tears – they'll make a delicious dressing for the grass you'll inevitably be eating tomorrow.

CAMOUFLAGE YOURSELF WITH TREE BARK

There are many predators in the forest, like particularly aggressive badgers, and doggers, so cover yourself in the bark of a tree to confuse them. If you are spotted, scare your predator by spreading your limbs to appear as large as possible and shrieking early Justin Bieber songs.

CAPTURE A PIG AND MAKE IT YOUR FRIEND

You are unlikely to meet other human beings in the forest because they have all decided to live in a warm house or apartment. But that doesn't mean you can't socialise! Capture a sheep or a pig from a nearby farm, draw a human face on it and tell it your problems. And like most people in real life, it won't be interested!

TURN YOUR FAECES INTO COMPOST

Don't waste a single nugget of your shit. Make a hole in the ground to relieve yourself in and then plant potatoes in it. It worked for Matt Damon in *The Martian* and he was on Mars! I don't know where you get the potatoes from in the first place, probably Notcutts Garden Centre. I know you're trying to avoid human contact but I've been round Notcutts a couple of times and you can hardly call the things that roam around in there human.

AND IF ALL ELSE FAILS . . . HAVE FOOD DELIVERED TO YOUR GPS COORDINATES

Sure, you're living in a forest under some damp leaves with only the sound of your own breath to entertain you, but if you have a sliver of phone battery left you can still order a takeaway. Many fast food restaurants now offer delivery to specific GPS locations, so just whack your details in and watch that Domino's driver lose his mind.

And there you have it – now you can live in the forest! It was nice knowing you, but it is a lot nicer knowing we'll never see you ever again!

ROSES ARE RED.
VIOLETS ARE BLUE.
I FORGOT YOU'RE ALLERGIC TO FLOWERS

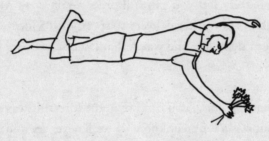

I'VE KILLED MY WIFE.

HOW TO
TACKLE FRAUD

In most circumstances, comedians make their living performing at various venues around the country. I say most because some of them make their money selling drugs, plus on occasion the gigs I've performed at can't reasonably be described as 'venues', more 'a space that the council would consider unfit for human inhabitants'. Most people choose to stage their comedy events in the evening, at around 8p.m., so a comic can only really do one or two performances in any one day. I did manage to do seven in a day at the Edinburgh Festival once – by the time I got on stage at the seventh show I was so tired and desensitised to being on stage that I basically had a nap mid-performance.

A few times a year, incredibly generous comedians like me will give up an evening of paid work to perform for free to raise money for a charitable cause. I know, I'm so kind and thoughtful, aren't I? Gosh, I'm a nice guy. And this is on top of all the imaginary work I do in the orphanage. The usual protocol is that you contact my agent, who will make you feel uncomfortable just for asking the question and then ask me, and if I'm free I'll probably say yes. Unless the charity is for something dumb like a local hospice or for children or something.

It emerged on Twitter that I was listed as performing at a charity gig that I'd never heard of after someone had messaged me saying it was appalling that I had 'bailed on a charity show for a television gig'. I was devastated because I would never do that – I would only cancel a charity gig for more money.

Whoever was organising the event had a professional(ish) poster produced with pictures of me, a couple of other acts (who knew nothing about the gig either), a venue, date and telephone booking number. The booking number was a mobile, so I decided to text it.

hello i want to buy tickets for the comedy night with joe licett are they still available? denise

Hi, I am so sorry but they are all sold out

OK is joe still on the bill im thinking of waiting at the venue for an autograph. denise

Sorry, no, all of the acts have changed for various reasons I am afraid.

OK ill wait outside just incase ill get there about 3 pm. denise

Why 3pm, the acts will not be there until 7?

Just to be safe don't want to miss them. denise

You will be wasting your time I am afraid as the acts never arrive before 7.

thats OK ill wait in my car. denise

OK, thank you for your interest, hopefully we will have a ticket spare for you.

I don't want a ticket ill just wait in my car. denise

As this exchange was happening I was simultaneously doing a bit of research into the gig, so don't ever tell me men can't multitask. Although I did have to put my phone down and do the research again because I couldn't focus on two things at once. The gig was presented as a one-off comedy night in a pub to raise money for a local care home, with all the acts donating their fee to the cause. This was apparently news to the care home, too. The mystery promoter, whoever it was, had obviously booked a load of local acts to fill out the bill, so that a comedy night did actually happen but not the one advertised. If you forget that it's false advertising and fraud, it's actually a sound business model. Did I mention if you go on my website you can buy tickets to 'Peter Kay'*?

---

* Peter Kay will not be appearing at the event in any capacity but I may eat some garlic bread.

My interest was piqued and I set a reminder on my phone for the day of the gig at 3p.m. The day came. The reminder pinged. I began to text.

> OK im here round the corner in my car are the acts there? denise

> No the acts aren't here they arrive 7pm.

> Is Joe Licett there yet? denise

> No, as I said, all the original acts had to cancel

> but it still says on his website he's going to be there. denise

> what?

> if you go on his website its listed there. denise

I've never been more delighted to be Joe Lycett than in this moment. Because I am me I can put up a fake gig on my website if I want to. I can do what I want. I can change my whole webpage to pictures of me in saucy poses if I want to. That's actually not a bad idea. But on this occasion for about ten minutes I was listed as being 'delighted to perform' at a fake gig.

As an aside, I should mention at this point that it was the closest I'd been to feeling like I've got split personality disorder, which I definitely don't/do have/haven't got/who are you? I felt a little bit like Denise was a real person, sat in a real car outside a gig that started in five hours, and I was taking time out of my busy comedian schedule to help her out. The harsh reality was I was in the bath watching *House of Cards*.

Also, if you happened to log onto my site for those ten minutes, I am very sorry if you bought tickets. How was the gig? Actually I don't need to ask. It was the best night of your sad little life.

I delighted at the fact that the guy must've been SO confused in that moment – maybe he had booked me? And forgot? Maybe that's how you book a comedian, just pretend you've booked them, and magically they come anyway?

There was a delay of about thirty minutes before the next reply, presumably as the guy cleared the shat from his pants.

> Sorry he must've forgotten to change it. Hes definitely not performing he cancelled for a paid gig.

This made me livid. How dare he claim I don't maintain my website properly. My main source of procrastinating is updating my website – I've just spent half an hour testing out how to arrange my saucy pics. In all seriousness, you'll know if I've got something incredibly important to work on, like my tax return or this book, because I'll have changed the font on my 'news' page.

It was time to go in for the kill. I wrote another message from 'Denise' designed to direct him back to my website for the final time.

> oh ive just refreshed his page its changed now. what a funny excuse he gives for cancelling! denise

I changed my webpage once more. On the 'live gigs' page I wrote: February 16th – DENISE DOESN'T EXIST.

OK I think you're Joe, im really sorry. There was a misunderstanding. Apologies for any confusion.

no its denise. denise

OK well apologies anyway.

can i have a ticket for the show? denise

I'll put one on the door for you.

HOW TO
BE INSPIRING
xoxo

Social media is a marvellous thing – imagine travelling back in time to tell your grandparents that in fifty years humans will be able to send a hate message to Amanda Holden whilst taking a dump. They'd be astonished and probably ask who Amanda Holden is. What a sensational world we live in.

Selfies, likes, favourites, retweets and rants are all now currency designed to boost followership in our brave new world and many awful celebrities are cashing in. But you're not a celebrity, you're probably just a pathetic teacher or doctor or something – your posts get completely ignored. Let's change that.

One way you can reverse your online anonymity is to get involved in a brand-new craze that is swamping celebrity social media accounts. In the hunt for more likes and faves, EVERYONE who is ANYONE is posting motivational but ultimately bullshit quotes! Got a lazy obvious catchphrase that means absolutely nothing? Perfect!

Here's how it works: an individual (usually a reality TV star or a pregnant teenager) will post a quote that they have stumbled across either elsewhere on social media or written on a toilet wall. These quotes differ wildly in content and style, but what they share is a *feeling* that they have some meaning or value – do not be fooled, they absolutely do not. Most of the time they'll be presented in a nice font, over a seascape background and accompanied by an addition from the postee such as 'omg so true' or 'I know some people who should read this!!!! You know who you are!!!! I'm talking about you Danielle!!!!'

Cheryl Cole/Fernandez-Virsini/Tweedy/Knobhead is one of the great innovators of this. One quote she posted provides a good introduction:

'Your attitude is your altitude – it determines how high you fly.' – anonymous

There's a reason no one has claimed authorship of that, Cheryl. Because it's dog shit. But who cares?! It got thousands of shares!

Other key contributors to this trend include model Cara Delevingne, TV presenter Laura Whitmore and the Kardashians. And they can all get in the fucking bin.

We are meant to glean from these quotes that the celebrities are intelligent, thoughtful and profound, despite the rest of their posts depicting vapid modelling shots or them looking sweaty and cross-eyed in the VIP area of Glastonbury Festival. You, the tiny idiot ant who follows them, are supposed to be enriched and improved by their generous post, a precious gift from the social media gods. How else are you supposed to know to 'Be Kind ;)' unless a bored and melancholy child of a millionaire has told you? The reality is the vast majority of their posts depict them in unattainably expensive clothes at parties you will never be invited to, all of which are intended specifically to exclude and undermine you.

After seeing this trend grow from a few high-profile key players to a full-on celebrity craze, I realised that there was no reason why normal people couldn't get in on the action – you're just as entitled to a piece of the pie as the Kardashians. Why should internationally famous models get all the likes? You can post a quote too!

If you want to grab this unique opportunity to grow your social media following, it is recommended you do some preliminary research. Have a look at what's being posted by the superstars and if you fancy it, start engaging! A good trick is to comment on some posts with additional thoughts or suggestions. Take this one, posted to Instagram by Cara Delevingne:

 **LISTEN & SILENT are spelt with the same letters.**
Think about it. ;)

What a brilliant post, Cara! I thought about this for about ten seconds and commented:

Also TINSEL. Think about that.
;)

You could've also had ENLIST or INLETS. Khloé Kardashian posted another quote that got me thinking:

We must learn who is gold and who is simply gold plated.

A good trick is to weigh them.

Sure, commenting on these is a lot of fun, but eventually you'll want to engage more. Comments get lost – you can't like or share a comment. Now is the time to start writing *your own* quotes!

It's important to find some inspiration for your first offerings. Mine were helped along after I stumbled across a post by someone who shall remain anonymous. No, actually I will name her because she used to call me fat at school even though she smelt like a Londis that's failed its hygiene standards test. Her name is Dani. She's since got fat herself and recently joined the Weight Watchers group on Facebook. Fuck you Dani, I win.

Her quote was thus:

4+3=7. But 5+2 also = 7.
Follow your own path.

My first thought was THIS IS SO TRUE. What amazing truths can be gleaned from maths, Dani. You can arrive at the same place via different routes! And for you, Dani, all those routes lead to a Nando's!

Dani's quote provided the springboard for my debut offering:

**Sometimes the self-service is no quicker than the normal checkout.
Follow your own path.**

I tagged Dani in the post, alongside Cheryl, Cara and the Kardashians. And it worked – it got dozens of likes and my profile jumped up by a massive THREE followers! So I did another:

**Sometimes the satnav hasn't updated yet and takes you down a road that doesn't exist any more.
Follow your own path.**

More likes, more popularity. My follower boost was now close to double figures. Success!

As you reach this point in your quote-writing career, you can start experimenting by posting completely original quotes. Remember, they should feel meaningful but actually mean absolutely nothing at all. And remember to keep them pithy, 'cause most people can't be bothered to read something longer than about ten words long. How you've got through this chapter is beyond me.

If you like, you can put the hashtag #bullshitquotesijustmadeup so people know that you're writing them. You're no copycat!

Don't cry when it rains. The weather is weeping for us all.

Feels nice, that. It means JACK SCHITT. It just fell out of my head.

Omg totes profound. Totes a load of bull I made up drunk.

I also did a sciency one:

In science, a negative attracts a positive. Which is why I think you're a twat.

And this seemingly profound bit of nothing:

Life is for the living. If you're not living, you're dead.

So there you have it, a guaranteed way to boost your followers on social media and garner the respect and admiration of your peers – as long as your peers are brain-damaged or in the fashion industry!

My favourite of my own quotes, you ask? Well, it's got to be the following:

Life is like a box of chocolates.
It doesn't last long if you're fat.

omg #sotrue hun xoxo

WHAT DO WE WANT!?
A CURE FOR ADHD!
WHEN DO WE WANT IT?!
LET'S PLAY SWINGBALL!

HOW TO
USE A SELFIE
AS A WEAPON

Travelling home late from a stand-up show on a Friday or Saturday night is a great time to play a fun game I like to call 'Vomit Roulette', an entertaining way to pass the time where you place bets with yourself as to who out of your fellow travellers is most likely to spew over themselves and/or other passengers. As with so many things in life, I've discovered it's the quiet ones you have to look out for – the ones retching loudly are more often than not mere attention-seekers. I've pitched 'Vomit Roulette' as a game to Hasbro – I've not yet heard back, but I think that might be because there is a typo in the document that suggests it would be suitable for ages 4+.

It was a cold Friday around 11p.m. when I boarded a train home from a perfectly pleasant show in Northampton. I scanned the carriage to assess where to sit – on one side was a small group of women dressed in hen attire, loudly sharing a bottle of vodka, a potential high-scoring group in any game of Vomit Roulette. At the opposite end of the carriage were a few quieter travellers. I decided the quiet end may be more palatable and sat myself down in the nearest available chair, opposite a gentleman whom I will henceforth call Wanky Peter. From the moment my buttocks graced the seat, Peter's eyes were piercing into me, an intensely sinister and aggressive stare. 'Maybe I am on fire,' I pondered to myself. He could've spotted something on my face perhaps, a large blemish or some rogue sauce, or maybe he was just admiring my skin, which I admit is plump and soft thanks to coconut oil and a daily nap. But after a solid five minutes, I was just freaking the hell out and wanted it to stop.

To give you a sense of what I was faced with, I should describe Peter. He was not an attractive specimen. A small man, pudgy, with thin spectacles and an old brown coat. He smelt of pork and a can of Lynx that had been bought in 2009. If I had to guess, I'd say he worked as a mortgage-broker for a small firm but had dreams of winning *Britain's Got Talent* with his pet dachshund. He's one of those guys who would have a little success flirting with a woman and then he'd lose confidence as he remembered that his penis looks like root ginger. I'm guessing – I didn't see his penis. Or at least that's what I'm going to write here.

My mind raced with possible solutions or escape routes but I was beginning to panic, and when I panic I do silly things. I once panicked in an Asda and bought seventy lemons. If I asked Peter to stop, it could start a conversation and I had over an hour left of my journey. I could move to the other end of the carriage with the hen party, but that would be chopping off my knob to spite my balls.

Then it came to me: give him something to stare at.

I have always taken great pleasure in how malleable my face is – I can squish and squash it into all sorts of hideous and remarkable shapes. In one moment I can look entirely normal, then suddenly I've made myself look like I've just come out of surgery for a lisp, or I suck my lips together so it appears the bone structure around my jaw has collapsed. Taking selfies of myself in these states is one of my absolute favourite things to do.

If you are a reader who does not understand the word 'selfie', let me reassure you that it is not as rude as it might sound – my mother used to think it meant pleasuring oneself, which is perfectly understandable for someone of her age. However, it does throw into question a lot of conversations we had where she just quietly nodded as I told her, 'I've been taking selfies with friends' or 'been teaching Grandad how to take a selfie'.

I started subtly, not making any sharp movements in order to ease Wanky Peter in without creating too much alarm . . .

. . . but gradually and confidently, I began to morph my face further . . .

. . . and further. Still Peter stared, now more than ever.

It wasn't working. If anything, he was enjoying it! I started panicking again, which manifested in involuntary weird noises. In the below photo, I'm making a noise in my throat that sounded a bit like a cat miaowing at high speed.

Despite all this, Peter refused to look away. His gaze was now more curious and constant than ever, his eyes perplexed. And yet I couldn't stop now – I was at maximum panic. In my despair, I decided to up the ante further. Courageously, I attempted to take my selfies whilst looking at him in his sinister pervy eye.

His confidence dropped . . .

. . . his eyes flickered away from mine for the first time, then back, then finally . . .

. . . he stopped and got off at the next stop.

And that is what is now known as **SELFIE-DEFENCE**.

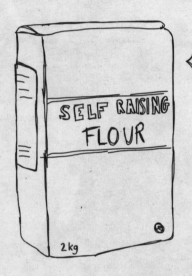

HOW TO
TAKE THE PERFECT
CELEBRITY SELFIE

From time to time, you may find yourself in the presence of a celebrity. It is probably less likely for you because you are not a celebrity (unless you are, in which case my Twitter account is @joelycett, please follow me) and so you are less likely to attract other celebrities. But if you do find yourself in that position, I know this is very hard but **do not panic.** They are just like you, exactly like you in every way apart from the fact they have a lot more money and friends and people will remember them after they die, unlike you who will be forgotten immediately.

Of course, when you meet a top sleb (as they're known) you will desperately want to take your picture with them, to show your other non-celebrity friends that you are better than them. But it is important to play it super cool and avoid looking like one of those awful wankers who takes pictures of themselves with famous people. There must be other ways to show Dani from school just how much more successful you've been since you graduated – and I don't mean passive-aggressively liking pictures of her gap year in India, even though it's clear to everyone she's a twat.

So how do you get a picture without looking like you want a picture? You don't ask them for a picture. You ask them if they want to be *art*.

I have created a USP (undeniably silly photograph) in the form of an art project called 'Always A Pleasure'. I will ask brazenly for a photograph with *anyone*, then reveal my special request – I demand that they look glum. The spiel goes something like this, 'Would you like to be part of an art project? All you have to do is take a photo with me but you must look like you are NOT happy to see me.' Then, when the picture is posted, I write a caption claiming that it is a great pleasure to see them. Now I can't be accused of being a brown-nosing showbiz wanker – I am an artist! What was once just a photo with me and Harry Styles is now an integral piece of a great masterpiece.

Here are some of my favourites from the series and of course, by 'favourites', I mean 'the ones the pencil-pushing bellend lawyers could get cleared'.

(At the end of this chapter you will find a handy 'make your own' Always A Pleasure with a space where you can cut out a picture of yourself and affix it to the page or, if you are a great illustrator like I have clearly demonstrated in this book, you could draw one in.

Remember to tweet it, Instagram it, Facebook it, WhatsApp it and don't forget to use the hashtag! Or don't do any of those things, because either way I really don't give a shit!)

~Always a pleasure to see Susan Calman~

The very first photo I took in this series. It will never be anything but an absolute pleasure to see Susan, as you can see very clearly here. We also have a rule where we have to wear effectively the same shirt every time we meet.

~Always a pleasure to see Joan Rivers~

Joan understood this concept faster than anyone I have ever attempted it with. I explained the premise and she just said, 'I'm not even going to look at you.' She'll always be one of the best.

~Always a pleasure to see Tom Daley~

Even when Tom is trying to look sad, he seems to remain chipper. It's probably all that clean living and chlorine poisoning.

~Always a pleasure to see the sea~

A stroll along the beach never fails to lift my spirits.

~Always a pleasure to see Kathy Burke~

I met Kathy on an appearance on *8 Out of 10 Cats Does Countdown* and we did this in one take, which is either testament to her exceptional acting abilities or a strong sign that I am genuinely unpleasant to be around.

~Always a pleasure to see Cuba Gooding Jr~

Cuba is one of the coolest people in showbusiness and as such was removed quickly by his management team when they saw this was happening.

~Always a pleasure to see my best friends on New Year's Eve~

One New Year's Eve all of my pals decided to take a selfie with a selfie stick, back when they were considered acceptable, but not one of them had noticed that I had retired to the bathroom. I returned to discover them mid-pic and was naturally devastated, before realising this was a perfect photo opportunity in itself.

~Always a pleasure to see Jimmy Carr~

Worryingly, I didn't even ask him to look unimpressed.

~Always a pleasure to see Gunner the Dog~

This, my friend Lara's dog, is one of the finest examples of why animals are far more intelligent than we give them credit for. I gave Gunner the spiel, as I do with everyone who I take these with, and he wasted not one moment in looking deeply unimpressed with everything about me.

~Always a pleasure to see Hayley Atwell~

Hayley is best known for her performance as the eponymous Agent Carter in the popular Marvel series, but I think her finest work is this picture.

~Always a pleasure to see Sarah Millican~

A great advocate of this idea, Sarah has a face that is normally so warm and kind and understanding that when she turns it to disgust, it cuts through you like a warm pen through cottage cheese.

~Always a pleasure to see Harry Styles~

This is one of ten billion pictures of Harry Styles in existence and I am proud to say it is probably the worst.

~Always a pleasure to see Amanda Holden~

I've never met Amanda and this is proof.

~Always a pleasure to see Edwina Currie~

Edwina Currie did not understand the brief.

Always a pleasure to see _____
#alwaysapleasure #parsnipsbuttered

A GIRAFFE'S NECK IS SO STRONG, A HUMAN COULD CLIMB UP IT.

ALSO, I'M BANNED FROM THIS SAFARI PARK.

HOW TO IMPROVE THE RAILWAYS

My despair and frustration at railway networks reaches back to before my birth. I think there was probably more than one occasion when I was in my mother's womb awaiting a fresh meal to be pumped down the umbilical cord, only to be forced to wait because the 17:04 was delayed due to an electrical fault and she needed to get home to cook and digest a halloumi sandwich. I demanded halloumi even from the womb.

My first foray into complaining to train companies took the form of an open letter to the head of Transport for London, which was incidentally published in *Time Out* magazine.

Dear TfL,
I have been travelling on your trains for a few years now and have some comments and recommendations that I think would benefit your service.

1. Firstly, I would like to contest the word 'tube'. This is a word normally reserved for containers of liquids or pastes and conjures thoughts of tomato purée, creams for rashes and used toilet rolls. A more accurate description of your service would be 'dirty cylinders'.
2. I am also against the use of the word 'oyster'. You are suggesting, I suppose, that with one of your cards 'the world is your oyster'. However, the card only works in London and so the metaphor is inaccurate. Unless it's called an Oyster card because of the smell of your trains, in which case, as you were.
3. Furthermore, a friend of mine visiting from overseas told his mother on the phone that he was 'getting on a tube with his oyster' and then spent the next fifteen minutes explaining that it wasn't a sexual reference or that London had turned him insane. Subsequently, your service did turn him insane.
4. I don't like the sort of people who hang around Camden station. Could you please have them removed?
5. The Bakerloo line is the colour of poo and thus I would like it changed to the Bakerpoo line for clarity.
6. Are all of your passengers balding? Because I see nothing but adverts for hair-loss centres. Is the quality of the air down there so thin that it's thinning our hair?
7. Elephant and Castle has no elephants or castles. Nor does Oxford or Piccadilly contain a circus. This is misleading and deeply upsetting.

8. Why does Monument/Bank have two names? Is it because bankers get off there and so, as usual, get more than the rest of us?
9. Fifty-five percent of the Underground is actually above ground. WTF guys?!
10. Finally, may I congratulate you on my favourite stations, which are 'Cockfosters', 'Mudchute', 'Bushey' and 'Swiss Cottage'.
Kind regards,
Joe Lycett

The response to the above was largely positive and I was inundated with tweets (I received two tweets) from fellow passengers, detailing their concerns and frustrations, which I of course did nothing about.

A while after, I discovered that Mark Carne, the acting CEO of Network Rail, has his email address publicly available online. As he is head of the organisation that owns all of the train stations in the United Kingdom, I would've thought he'd known better than to make this information public, but alas now I had it and you know what that means.

My initial email was sparked by the most irksome of Network Rail policies . . .

Dear Mark Carne,
I am contacting you regarding an urgent emergency at London Euston and figured, as CEO of Network Rail, you may be able to help.
Last night I enjoyed a prawn masala and garlic naan from a curry house in Peckham. I had concerns about the hygiene

standards of the establishment but my hunger was such that I chose to ignore the warning signs. Thus today I have been, as my father would say, 'pissing through my arse'.

The reason this is relevant to you is that I currently find myself at London Euston train station without 30p. As your toilet facilities demand this fee and I am about to explode I am left in quite the quandary! I have managed to find some privacy and am currently perched behind a bin on one of the platforms near Delice de France, desperately trying to hold in what I anticipate to be an absolute cascading waterfall of post-masala shit.

I was wondering if you might be able to lend me some of your £675,000 salary (or 2,250,000 train station toilet trips per annum – you lucky bugger!) to avoid this impending disaster. Either that, or perhaps stop charging for what most people would consider to be a basic human right.

I await your reply, eagerly.

Regards,

Joe Lycett

P.S. Should you lend me the money I would be delighted to invite you for tea at my home to say thank you, but please give me plenty of notice as I will need to install a turnstile outside the bathroom before your arrival.

P.P.S. You're literally taking the piss

I cannot be sure it is my influence, but a few months after the above email was sent, Birmingham's new train station and shopping centre, Grand Central, were opened. It shares only a name with New York's famous station – walking through the interior is like being encased in a giant egg. They sell halloumi wraps in one of the shops there, so I don't care. But the main thing is this: the toilets are free. I see this as a small but important victory.

Regardless, Mark Carne never replied. Days passed. The days turned into weeks, the weeks into months. I oft thought of Mark, about how snubbed I felt by him, how cruel he'd been in his silence. I wondered if he ever thought of me. Then one night in late summer, after a few Lambrinis, I snapped and sent him another email.

Dear Mark,

I contacted you many months ago about an unfortunate situation I had in London Euston where I needed to use the lavatory but didn't have the required funds. I am still yet to receive a reply but I imagine that is because you intended to reply to me at 12:04 but then got slightly delayed 'til 12:06, then delayed further to 12:20 and ultimately decided to cancel entirely, with little regard for me and my life and no apology. You will be pleased to know I have since incinerated the trousers I was wearing that day and murdered all witnesses. I thank you for your stoic silence in this matter.

Now I have your email address, I thought I might offer some guidance on how to improve Network Rail and the rail service in the United Kingdom in general. I have set out my suggestions below, which I hope you will act on without delay, although I know you struggle with the phrase 'without delay'.

- Rail fares should not represent the length of the journey but the quality of the destination. For example, a trip to beautiful rural Yorkshire might cost you £40, whereas a trip to Milton

Keynes should cost 40p. People should be completely reimbursed for all travel if they chose to leave Coventry.

- London Victoria should be burnt to the ground and you should start again.

- 'Mind the gap' is a confusing phrase – imagine trying to translate that for a French tourist? It should be replaced with something like, 'Look Out There Is A Big Fucking Hole Between The Train And The Platform And Should You Fall In We Will Continue Regardless Cause We're Already Delayed'.

- Before every Virgin train leaves the platform, I'd like there to be a thin sheet that the train has to drive through, known as 'the train hymen'. Independent hymen verifiers will not let the train depart until they are convinced the carriages are clean and the card machine is working in the shop. Only then will they shout, 'I DECLARE THAT THIS TRAIN IS VIRGINAL' and it is free to depart.

- You should change your name from Mark Carne so as to not get confused with Mark Carney, the Governor of the Bank of England. I suggest just referring to yourself as 'The King of Trains'.

- Wi-fi should be free to everyone on trains, not just first class. And it should be called Wi-Dial-Up to accurately describe the speed. Oh! Now I know why you didn't reply to my last email! It's still downloading! Alas, you'll probably receive this email in the fourth millennium.

Thank you and goodbye forever,

Joe Lycett

P.S. I have attached a flattering drawing I just did of what I think you look like naked.

A reply to this has also failed to materialise, so I am in the process of pitching the above image as Network Rail's new logo. Watch this space.

TOLD MOTHER I WAS HAVING A
'LAMB SHANK'. SHE SAID, 'THAT
SOUNDS LIKE A WEIRD SEX ACT!'

I LAUGHED AND STARTED FUCKING
THE LAMB.

HOW TO
IMPROVE WAITROSE

My local supermarket in Birmingham is a Waitrose. There's a common stereotype that the people who inhabit Waitrose are posh and stuck-up and spend too much money on stuff they could get a lot cheaper elsewhere. And that stereotype is absolutely bang on the money, well done whoever said that.

I wouldn't normally choose to go to Waitrose but it's my local, so I am forced to endure it against my will. I definitely wouldn't drive a further fifteen minutes to go there over, say Aldi, which is a perfectly good supermarket. Instead, my cross to bear is suffering the indignity of helpful staff and good-quality, overpriced, fresh produce. It is an unbearable horror. Gosh, I am such a saint.

The clientele of Waitrose is well documented as being middle class to the point of ridiculous. On one occasion, I found myself in the fresh bread aisle of my local store, perusing the sweet-smelling loaves that had just been removed from the oven. My eye perchanced upon a particularly delicious-looking dome of sourdough and I did not wait a moment to plunge my hand in to the plastic compartment to capture it. No sooner had I prised it from its container and placed it in a bag than a small, impeccably dressed elderly woman emerged from nowhere, and immediately barked at me: 'You should use the tongs for that!' I admit I had not used the provided tongs to handle the loaf but I had a perfectly good reason for this. I looked back at her and explained that I had failed to use the implement as it would only be me who would be handling and eating the bread from this point forward.

'Well, I didn't know that, did I?' she snapped back.

'Well, I didn't know I was going to be interviewed by the Tong Police, did I?' was my riposte.

The woman shook her curls (I presume she used some other tongs on those!) as if to despair at all the people younger than her in the world, merely because I hadn't used a tong to get hold of a sourdough loaf. She's a regular at my Waitrose, and if we are ever both in there at the same time I make a point of running my fingers gently along the tops of each of the loaves, with no desire other than to make her produce hot steam from her ear canals.

There are many improvements that could be made in Waitrose.*
Whatever, I'm not ashamed. For example, I have thought for
some time now that someone should be employed to police the
car park, particularly focussing on stopping people in 4x4s
parking across two spaces. Perhaps you need a giant car to protect
a child you are chauffeuring, or maybe the back seat is good for
naps – whatever the reason, I don't care, make it fit in a designated
parking bay, or walk. As you well know, dear reader, I am very
concerned that people park in an orderly manner and would
never condone people breaking the rules.

They could also do with improving some of their products and
so I have taken it upon myself to pen a couple of letters to them,
explaining my deep concerns. If I'm going to have to sell Mother's
jewellery to buy a sandwich, I'm expecting superior quality.

The first is a letter I wrote to them when they introduced the
pork and Bramley apple sausage roll. I cannot begin to explain
to you how excited I was about this addition to my life. Sausage
rolls are one of the finest inventions in human history, as are
sausages with apple in them, so this new development had the
potential to be groundbreaking. Sadly, it was not to be, and I
penned this short complaint.

Dear Mr Waitrose,
I am an avid Waitrose supporter and very
much enjoy shopping in your stores. I have
a store close to my home but also do a lot
of driving and have started shopping for
'driving snacks' at your stores at select motorway service stations.
On a recent trip to one such store I was delighted to see on
sale a pack of two pork and Bramley apple sausage rolls. I am a

*I understand this is totally the sort of thing the stuck-up opinionated tossers
who shop at Waitrose would say but alas I am one of them.

big fan of sausages with Bramley apple (they make a quite delicious toad-in-the-hole) and enjoy things in pairs, so I thought that this was, quite frankly, **a stroke of pure genius.** I purchased a packet immediately and ran back to the car with the excitement of a child on Christmas morning.

But, like most Christmases, the excitement was short-lived.

The sausage was, as expected, delicious. The addition of the Bramley apple remains a sensation and you should be applauded for this. I am applauding you currently in my conservatory. But the pastry. What a travesty! Putting aside the grotesque volume of pastry, it was impossibly dry, spoiling what should have been a pleasant and moist experience. Ginsters have nothing as promising in concept as your idea, but their execution is far superior.

I have some suggestions:

1) Reduce the amount of pastry considerably. There should be substantially more sausage than roll.

2) Improve the recipe of your pastry. More moisture is required.

3) On completing suggestions 1 and 2, take a week off and watch the money roll in!

I hope you can implement these improvements. Trust me, you won't look back! If you don't implement them, I cannot promise that I will not start up a rival company specialising in Bramley apple sausage rolls, although this is very unlikely as I am not a good businessman, my passion for this topic extends about as far as this email and I am already quite busy.

Have an absolutely smashing day!

Regards,

Joe Lycett

To their unending credit, Waitrose responded to this letter with a letter of their own, apologising for the 'distress' (great word) their product had caused me and offering me £4 in vouchers. Now whilst this sounds good in principle, £4 translates to around 0.74 slices of bread by their prices. This was a foolish move on their part. I expect they thought vouchers would get rid of me, as they would with most people, but this only encouraged me to write further.

I had another concern that had been festering for some time. One of my main gripes with Waitrose's products is their misuse of the English language to describe them. More than most, they are prone to hyperbole or just plain inaccuracy. For example, I know of no human, living or dead, who would use the word 'majestic' to describe a bunch of basil or demand that their eggs be laid by hens with 'an inquisitive nature'. They also have their 'essentials' range, which stretches the definition of the word to breaking point. The range is akin to Sainsbury's Basics or Tesco Value but, whereas these offerings are for things that are actually basic or value, the Waitrose Essentials range includes things such as 'marinated artichoke hearts'. Excuse me? Who considers these to be 'essential', other than some overpaid middle-class inheritance-guzzling sponge? Oh I see, that's your clientele. As you were.

Which brings us neatly to the 'perfectly ripe' avocado. I love an avocado, particularly if it's mashed onto some bread. They're a relatively healthy and delicious treat. But getting them on the right day is one of life's near impossibilities, as they remain unripe for weeks and then ripen unannounced and stay edible for about ten seconds, before becoming brown and putrid. Waitrose claims to have removed this concern from life by proudly selling them at their ripest, but this is all too often not the case. I put finger to keyboard and complained once more.

Hello Waitrose,

I am writing to you to offer my services in regard to your 'perfectly ripe' avocados. I would like to dispute your definition of 'perfectly ripe' – I think you have mistaken the word 'perfectly' for the word 'not'. If this is in fact the correct definition I apologise and I am 'perfectly' a virgin.

I have generously taken time out of my busy day of not eating avocados to compile a list of things you may suggest to your customers they use them for, instead of as a delicious accompaniment to a salad or crushed and spread onto bread:

- Paperweight.
- As a replacement hammer.
- Refined to a point and placed at the end of a spear.
- Inserted into a catapult to demonstrate medieval warfare.
- Used alongside a thick ceramic bowl as a makeshift pestle and mortar.
- Placed into the pockets of canal-boat dwellers you wish to drown.

Should you wish, I am happy to loiter next to your avocados and explain the options to passing customers for the small fee of £10,000.

Please let me know how you'd like to proceed.

Many thanks,

Joe Lycett

P.S. Your name for 'spring onions' is 'salad onions'. Why? Literally no one calls them this. Anyway, I found them for a pound cheaper in Aldi and it gave me a real salad in my step.

Confusingly, no reply. Too far? Probably too far.

THIS CHOCOLATE
MOUSSE I
FOUND IN A
BAG IN THE
PARK TODAY
TASTES A
LOT LIKE
DOGSHIT.

HOW TO SELL A STORY TO A NEWSPAPER

One of my favourite things to do on a rainy day is to use one of my aliases to send emails to newspapers claiming to have a sensational celebrity story. You might say that this is a weird pastime but I bet you do weirder stuff, like horse riding or volunteering for a charity or something. God, you're such a little square, sitting at home reading a book. You should get out more.

Some of the stories I've attempted to sell include:

Photographs of Amanda Holden climbing through the window of a Pret A Manger.

Evidence that Ainsley Harriott is having an affair with Clare Balding.

Uncovered documents purporting to show that Gillian McKeith has tried to copyright the word 'poo'.

Photographs taken in Wickes of Samantha Mumba buying 300 saws.

Long-lens photographs of Simon Cowell outside the X *Factor* studios eating a raw carrot.

Pictures of Cara Delevingne in the front seat of a Vauxhall Astra Uber sticking her tongue out at the driver.

Blurry photographs of *Great British Bake Off* star Paul Hollywood punching a cat.

It's essential when selling a fake story that you select the right level of celebrity. The higher their profile, the more likely the press already know exactly what your chosen celeb is doing at all times – the lower the profile, the less likely they are to give a shit. Much as I love Alison Hammond, the tabloid press clearly don't care that I saw her 'selling duty-free cigarettes in a nursery school car park'.

My celebrity of choice: Matt Baker, host of BBC One's *The One Show*.

I've tried to sell SO many stories about him. He's one of those celebrities who everyone knows and yet no one really knows at all. He used to present children's television. He's got dogs. There's a sadness about him, a sort of blind hope that everything will be OK. I bet he's a bit lonely. I bet he doesn't really drink and gets tired at 9:30p.m. I bet Alex Jones invites him out after every recording of *The One Show* and he says something like, 'I'd love to but I'm defrosting a lamb shank.'

I think the beauty of Matt Baker is that in a weird way anything could be believable, anything is possible. When I was younger, he was always trying out some whacky new activity on children's television – he'd be hang-gliding one week, making his own cheese the next. This has meant that I can imagine him doing pretty much anything. Like hover-boarding through a council estate. Or slaughtering a pig on his farm. Or getting caught buying lube in bulk. Or murdering a postman. It's all possible!

So I sent an email to all the tabloids, under the guise of my alias Paul Paulington, claiming to have pictures of him kicking a pigeon. An unexpected but believable story. The folks employed by the tabloid press are some of the sharpest and most astute people you are likely to come across. Thus most of my attempts are snubbed or ignored pretty early on and, as such, many of them ignored my emails about this specific pigeon-kicking incident. Except the *Sun*. Their newsdesk replied within minutes and seemed genuinely thrilled at the prospect of taking Mr Baker down a peg or two.

But it wasn't that simple . . .

From: *Paul P*

To: *Sun Newsdesk*

Subject: *Exclusive photo for sale*

To the editor,

     I was recently strolling through London when I spotted Matt Baker from the BBC One Show on his phone in the street. There was a pigeon on the pavement and at one point he was so angry that, to my amazement, he tried to kick the pigeon. He had about three attempts and on one of them he did clip its wing. He was shouting what sounded like, 'Die, pigeon prick.'

     I managed to get some pictures. I was wondering how much you might be interested in buying them for?

Regards,

Paul P

Not one to miss out on a scoop, I got the following reply within three minutes.

From: *Sun Newsdesk*

To: *Paul P*

Paul,

     Kicking a pigeon? That is pretty shitty for a One Show bloke. Can you send me the pictures?

    Cheers,

Graham Gregory (I've changed his name for legal reasons)

Sun Newsdesk

I'd say using the phrase 'pretty shitty' is pretty colloquial for a first email back.

To my knowledge, no pictures of Matt Baker kicking a pigeon actually exist, which I find very upsetting, but this meant I was forced to improvise.

From: *Paul P*
To: *Sun Newsdesk*

Graham,
    My lawyer says I shouldn't send you the full pictures until I have an offer from you about how much you will pay for them. I have attached a cropped version of one of the shots for the time being.
Regards,
Paul P

That image is literally what you get when you do a Google search for the word 'pigeon'. I find the weird bit of gunk on the ground next to it disconcerting.

From: *Sun Newsdesk*
To: *Paul P*

That's a photo of a pigeon.
Here's my photo of a pigeon.
Graham

I absolutely loved that Graham was playing along. I think I sort of fell for Graham at that moment. I expect if I ever meet him I'll go all shy, try to impress him with a uninteresting anecdote and then beg he follows me on Twitter.

We couldn't have the fun ending there, so I replied a little more forcefully.

From: *Paul P*
To: *Sun Newsdesk*

Yes, Graham. The question is, how much are you willing to pay for a photo of Matt Baker kicking that pigeon?
Regards,
Paul P

Because sure, we were all having a lot of fun, but I had a 'serious' 'business' 'proposal'.

Here's a picture of Matt Baker. Can you send me a picture of this man kicking a pigeon?
Graham

Oh, look at lovely Matt Baker. He seems like he has a warm heart and soft hands. Plus he once asked David Cameron, 'How do you sleep at night?' on an episode of *The One Show*. He's a cool guy. I bet in this picture he's just on his way home to cook his lamb shank. That's not a euphemism. Unless you want it to be.

Graham,

I feel you are not taking me seriously. Anyone can Google a picture of a pigeon or Matt Baker. I should tell you the **Guardian** have made a firm offer on this.

Regards,

Paul P

Paul,

I worry the **Guardian** may not be taking you seriously, since they have a clear and firm editorial policy of never paying for stories.

However, the **Sun** does pay for stories and we are deadly serious about this.

If you have clear, printable pictures of Matt Baker from **The One Show** kicking a pigeon in a public place – a very antisocial and alarming way to behave, inevitably in front of children – then I believe we would be comfortable offering £1,000 for those images.

Of course, I cannot make a firm offer until I have actually laid eyes on these photographs.

How would you like to respond to this?

Graham

My favourite sentence in the above is 'inevitably in front of children'. Why is Graham making up new details about a story that doesn't even exist?

As I said, the journalists at the tabloids are shrewd operators and Graham's clearly one of the shrewdest. He might actually be a shrew. I didn't know the *Guardian* don't pay for news stories, an essential bit of knowledge, which I should have been aware of.

I was on the back foot. The only way to respond was with a curveball.

Is that a picture of Matt Baker? I thought he
was Chinese.
Regards,
Paul P

 You thought he was Chinese? You mean you have a
picture of a Chinese man kicking a pigeon?

I do actually have one of these.

Yes. How much will you pay for it?

Regards,
Paul P

 I fear we might be wasting each other's time.
Good day.
Graham

Graham,
You'll be sorry when you see tomorrow's
Guardian front page.
Good day.
Paul P

 I usually am.

HE'S MAKIN' A LIST,
HE'S CHECKIN' IT TWICE.
HE'S CHECKIN' IT AGAIN.

HE'S HAVING ANOTHER LOOK.

SANTA CLAUS HAS CRIPPLING OCD

HOW TO
SURVIVE
CHRISTMAS

I'll be honest – I'm not the biggest fan of Christmas. It's dark, it's damp, everywhere is busy and turkey is a shit meat.

This hasn't always been the case. As a boy, I used to find the anticipation of Christmas Day arriving the most exciting and thrilling time of the year. I couldn't wait for Santa Claus to drop off his delivery. Now, I can't make a comment about Santa Claus 'dropping off his delivery' without thinking it's some sort of euphemism. Whereas before I would welcome the first flakes of snow on a crisp winter morning, these days as the Yuletide season approaches I begin to tense up, I become irritable and I brace for attack. I also think 'Yuletide' sounds like a sex act. I don't know what, but something involving a log. Alas, my childhood is ruined.

I can pinpoint the exact moment when Christmas lost its sheen for me. It was late afternoon on Christmas Eve a few years back and I was finishing up a last-minute shopping spree – I always do my shopping the day before, and sometimes the evening before, which is why everyone got a gift from 24hr-Tesco in 2012. I rushed back to my car weighed down by a hundred poorly considered presents to discover I had received a gift of my own. The cruellest of gifts: a parking fine. This was the genesis of my hatred for traffic wardens and the death of Christmas.

I had presumed, erroneously, that Christmas Eve was a bank holiday. Even if it wasn't, I couldn't comprehend how anyone could be so callous as to issue a parking fine on the most exciting of holy days. I was fortunate, as I could afford to pay it – I am Joe Lycett, star of show business, after all – but what if this fine had been handed out to a poorer individual, one who could not afford it? I could not stand for this gross misuse of power.

I was new to letter-writing at this time, and in hindsight I realise I perhaps went in too hard. Friends of mine reassured me that the fucking piece of shit wankers at the council deserved my initial greeting to them, but when I read it back now I realise my opening line may have lost me some respect.

Dear Bastards,

I got a parking ticket in Birmingham City centre on 24th December 2011. You may be familiar with this date's more popular name, Christmas Eve.

I was in town buying food and toys for some sick and starving children I look after in a local orphanage, plus a small gift for my dear old mother (some novelty chocolates in the shape of male genitalia, aptly named Cocklates).

When I returned to my car, you can imagine my surprise and disappointment to find a parking ticket affixed to the windscreen. I cried, as Jesus did on Christmas Day, 'Forgive these sinners, they know not what they do.' I may have also chased your parking enforcement officer down the road shouting, 'DIE JUDAS.'

I am willing to offer, as payment, a bottle of sherry. If you refuse this offer, I will have to pay the fine using money from the orphanage, which will force me to starve one of the weaker children. His name is Graham (picture attached) and he is a 6-year-old boy with fair hair and the voice of an angel – doctors tell me that without food he will not make it through the winter.

Regards,

Joe Lycett

P.S. Mother very much enjoyed the Cocklates. She was quite surprised by the coconut filling!

P.P.S. Just to be absolutely clear: if you do not cancel the fine, I will kill a child.

The photograph above is not, as stated, a picture of a young starving child called Graham but an adorable snap of me as a boy. A time when I had smooth skin and hope in my eyes. Now, I look more like a bag of out-of-date yoghurt that's been left in a van. That's what a lifetime of parking fines will do to you.

I received no reply to my complaint, only adding to the sense that Christmas had abandoned me. My only solace was that I made it into the *Birmingham Mail* in an article with the following title:

Booze Offer for Parking Fine Is a No Go For Joe

I do love the *Birmingham Mail*.

As with all articles in the *Birmingham Mail*, it was a fantastic, thrilling read. Like a true narcissist, my favourite extract in the article is a quote from myself, in which I explain my follow-up threat:

On failing to get a response after 14 days, 23-year-old Joe wrote again to the council: 'The lack of closure is making this whole thing unendurable.

'As you did not accept my offer of a bottle of sherry, it has now been reduced to a half bottle. In fact, it is more like a third of a bottle as Mother had a bit too much on account of her finishing both the whisky and the gin.'

I was pleased with that.

Foolishly, I had thought that this was merely a small blip in my enjoyment of Christmas, but I couldn't have been more mistaken. My festive parking fine was but the tip of the iceberg of annoyances and irritations to come. And somehow, year on year, turkey becomes a shitter meat.

A troubling trend emerged around this time, which began as a fun little novelty some families participated in but which is now a full-on pandemic. I am referring to The Christmas Newsletter. Every December, the Lycett family is inundated with this propaganda (sometimes up to three letters!) from families we sort of know proudly listing the many achievements of their children. Part of me likes the dull voyeurism of reading them but it's the same part of me that likes to get naked and watch the old man across the road through a slit in the curtain. I don't actually do that, I just want him to read this and think I do it. Just have a look now, Barry. See that eye in the upstairs bedroom. THAT'S MY EYE, BARRY.

One particular 'family friend'* (*I use quote marks here because we haven't actually seen this family for over a decade and have had no contact with them on account of the restraining order) who will remain anonymous (I'll call her Debrah, because that is actually her name) has an  unbecoming habit of not only telling us that her two children have been promoted in their law firms but also explaining that they are earning more money by using exact figures. I'm thrilled Marcus is doing well, but do I need to know he's earning £125,000 with the promise of a bonus? No. Shit off Debrah, the main thing I remember about Marcus is that he had ugly shins.

Last year, her newsletter spanned two pages of double-sided A4 in Times New Roman – a heinous excuse for a font. Incidentally the publishers of this book tried to convince me to use Times New Roman. Some of that correspondence was good fun. Apparently 'Gary in the graphics department is signed off with stress' because 'the card you sent him with each letter in a different font to "show variety" gave him heart palpitations.' Get well soon, Gary!

Debrah's crime was not just Times New Roman, but the ghastly content of the letter too. It included passages like this: 'Sarah has been house-hunting with her partner Dan for the last 3 months and they think will settle for a small cottage 2 miles outside Oxford valued at £895,000. They've been saving for the last five years and have managed to sort out a deposit of around £100,000 which should get them a more desirable mortgage.'

TOO MANY NUMBERS, DEBRAH.

I ignored all of Debrah's letters every year until the temptation to send my own, SUPER-DAFT newsletter became too much and I fired off the below. I deliberately filled it with a sarcastic amount of numbers and addressed it to 'all' to make it appear like it was a round robin.

But I only sent it to Debrah.

Hello All,

It's been 12 months or 52 weeks or 365 days since last Christmas and such a lot has happened!

THE YEAR IN STATS: I've had 0 children, proposed 0 times, been to 5 weddings, 6 funerals, had 7 fights, taken 365 naps (one a day), gained 9,000 instagram followers and eaten 20,000 slices of halloumi (approx.).

Mother and Father are happy and healthy – they spent something in the region of £4,500 buying a log burner, which pumps out about 8kW of heat and has reduced their energy bills by 23 per cent. They love it and have already burned through around 400 logs in about 8 weeks. They've set fire to the house or themselves approximately 18 times!

I went on 3 holidays this year because I'm 27 and I can do what I like. The first, to Lanzarote, was all-inclusive and I think I must've vomited about 100 times from overeating. It's built on a volcanic island – Father said he went there when he was younger and remembered the 'lovely black beaches'. Mother misheard him, which caused some confusion for a while. He turns 66 next year, if Mother doesn't kill him before.

Things are steady with work and I am pleased to be writing a book. It's a sort of manual to modern life, which contains not one piece of actual proper advice. It'll be on sale for about £20 next Christmas. I'd like to sell over 50,000 copies – about 49,000 will just be copies Mum purchases to send to friends and family!

At the start of the year, I had an insatiable desire to have sex and ended up sleeping with probably about 3 men and 4 women. One of the suitors, Pedro, was sensational – I don't wish to be crass but it was 5-star sex. He just had a way with his body, like it was an ethereal entity separate from him and yet intrinsically part of us both. We must've seen one another only 12 times before I discovered he was a fan of Jeremy Clarkson and ended it. The phase has passed and I'm now just alone in a one bed flat.

Next year I am hoping to save up £1,000,000 to buy a small cupboard to live in around Central London.

All our love,

Joe Lycett (27) & The Lycett Family (collective age: 164)

P.S. One more thing: Nan died.

P.P.S. I've attached a recent picture of myself.

(NB: As a little joke to myself, if you add up all the numbers mentioned in the letter you get the number 1,134,206. If you type this into a calculator and turn it upside down, it spells GO 2 HELL.)

If she doesn't get the message and sends me another one next year, I will be designing a whole pamphlet outlining the life histories of every member of my family and every person of every family I've met. That'll show her. Or maybe I'll just ignore it and not make such a big deal of it. But that's my decision and mine alone to make.

Many of you may be wondering, 'Joe, you're clearly a bit of a Grinch. Is there truly nothing about Christmas that you enjoy?' I refuse to answer that question. What I will tell you is my absolute least favourite thing about modern attempts to celebrate the birth of Jesus, our lord and saviour and something. My least favourite thing is the prevalence of German Christmas markets.

Every winter Birmingham city centre (my beloved home town) becomes awash with bored Germans in wooden huts thanks to the German Christmas market craze, an absolute swipe of shite devised to make you pay a £2 deposit for a glass in which to put a half pint of warm £4 beer. It's ugly and smelly and noisy. It drags people away from local businesses. I didn't mind it at first as it was contained to one area but now it stretches its sauerkraut sausage tentacles along almost every street in the city centre, bringing with it a load of opportunistic irks drinking mulled wine in the street while I try desperately to buy last-minute gifts.

This isn't me being xenophobic by the way – I like Germany a lot, I think it's a cool country with an amazing, complex history. Berlin is one of my favourite cities in the world. But the market is not representative of Germany in any way. Thinking you've had an authentic German experience by eating a sausage at the

German Christmas market is like thinking you're the King when you've shagged a waxwork of the Queen.

I wanted to write to Birmingham City Council about the market but I've burned quite a few bridges with them as a result of complaining weekly about fly-tipping in my local area, and by calling them 'bastards' when they gave me that Christmas Eve parking fine. I still stand by that. Thus, I felt emailing from myself on this occasion could potentially be the straw that breaks the camel's pretzel-covered back. Instead, I posed as none other than Chancellor of Germany, Angela Merkel or 'Angie M', as I decided she refers to herself.

I made a point of using the word 'knob' as much as possible – *knoblauch* means garlic in Germany and I find this hysterical because I am an adult child, naturlich.

From: Angie Merk
To: Birmingham City Council
Subject: Frankfurt Christellnacht Market

Guten Tag Birmingham City Council,
Ich would like to tachen this opportunity to congratulate you on your Frankfurt Christellnacht market. As the Chancellor of Deustchland, I, Angela Dorothea Merkel, am thrilled with what you have achieved. It is sehr gut to see the German knoblauchbrot being sold on every strasse in Birmingham – I love a bit of knob auf mein brot.

Whilst ich love what you've done with the plasse, Ich habe some suggestions:

- Make it sehr bigger. It ist not imposing enough auf das town centre.
- Change das market currency to das euro.

- Ban David Cameron. Ich think he ist ein twat.

- Can du sell some colourful suits like ich wear auf das European Parliament so ich becommen eine fashion ikon. Ich habe a gut supplier.

- Ich want to see all das local businesses on das high strasse to close as a result of das Christellnacht Market.

- More knob auf mein brot.

Please act auf meine suggestions immediately. Danke for your time, bitte.

Auf wiedersehen,
Angie M.
xoxo

For reasons I will never fully understand, I received no reply to this.

Despite all my frustrations with Christmas I would still like you to have a good time, honest. It can be the most magical and wonderful time of the year. An opportunity to give something special to someone you love. There is no greater feeling in the world than watching as they unwrap the gift you have spent hours deliberating over, peeling back the tissue paper to reveal a beautiful cashmere jumper. It's a high-quality, expensive piece by a top end designer, a deep blue, their favourite colour. Your heart fills with warmth as they look back to you, the light of their life, a tear in their eye at your gesture.

They take your hand in theirs and say to you, 'XXL? What the fuck are you trying to say? I've been swimming three times a week all year and you buy me XXL? What a fucking cheek.'

Merry Christmas.

HOW TO CONTEST A PARKING FINE

Motoring is an expensive endeavour – there's road tax, insurance, fuel, and that's before you've even thought about investing in a beaded chair back or a portable heated coffee cup. Then, after you've shelled out for all that, you leave your vehicle slightly over a double yellow line and some jobsworth in a shit hat leaves a note on your dashboard saying you owe him £60. Curiously they never leave a name, always hiding behind their 'parking enforcement officer number', because they are withering, pathetic cowards.

The fines themselves seem to be arbitrarily decided by each local council, with most opting for that most transparent of bargains: 'It's £60 reduced to £30 if you pay in 14 days.' What nonsense. It's nothing more than a way to make themselves seem generous and compassionate. The reality is it's £30, which then doubles if you don't pay in 14 days. That's like me saying, 'If you call my mum a slag I'll kill you, but if you just say she's a tart I'll reduce it to GBH.' Whichever way you look at it, you're ruining my day and Mum's still a tart.

I have been told that I should pity parking enforcement officers, that their jobs are difficult and tedious, that they must 'get a lot of flak'. I assure you I would spend some time pitying them if I wasn't so busy trying to utterly destroy their lives. I have no pity for them, nor should anyone. One should reserve no patience for people in professions whose job satisfaction is achieved by ruining someone else's day. I am convinced they know they are doing wrong. These little rats hide in the shadows – when have you ever met someone at a party who admitted, 'I work as a parking enforcement officer'? Never. Because why would you tell a stranger that you have the moral compass of a landmine?

My ire for these opportunistic-daylight-robbing pigs exists because I get an unusual number of parking fines. I do a considerable amount of driving on account of my job and regularly arrive late and flustered regularly. Plus I am bad at parking, all of which creates the ideal conditions for a parking enforcement officer to descend from whichever rotten crack they reside in and give me a fine. Who knew just leaving it on the M42 was illegal?!

One of my first ingenious tricks to avoid parking fines was to keep hold of one of the little plastic bags they put the fine into, which I would then affix to my windscreen whenever I felt I was parked illegally, so as to make it appear that I had already received a fine. However this loophole was short-lived as, much to my chagrin, they developed some sort of digital system that could tell them whether I had actually been administered a fresh fine, rendering the technique useless. Also, I made the schoolboy error of using Birmingham City Council parking fine bags whilst parked illegally in Shrewsbury.

After some extensive research, I stumbled across the holy grail of complaining, the finest and most useful bit of law you are ever likely to encounter. It is known as the Subject Access Request and is part of the Data Protection Act 1998. I know this because I have a lot of spare time on my hands.

A Subject Access Request is a formal request you can make to any institution or company asking for any personal data that they hold on you. It is within your rights to see a copy of anything that they have on you. This is useful because it is a phenomenal waste of a local council's time – no one's real dream was to end up working in the parking office, if you're there you've failed at something, and as such the vast majority of people that take these jobs generally want to coast along unperturbed until 5p.m. In my experience, if you overwhelm them with admin, more often than not they will buckle and cease their harrassment.

Whilst my main use is for parking fines, this fabulous technique can be used to annoy a whole variety bucket of individuals and institutions. The beauty of it is that once the request is made, there is very little wriggle room for the receiver to get out of it. They can ask for a small admin fee but it can only be nominal, they can ask for further information as to the specific information you require but they cannot ask why you are asking for the information or what you are going to do with it. If they don't respond to your request, they are breaking the law and you could take them to court. In many ways, my ultimate life dream is to take an entire local council to court and have them all sent to jail just because they didn't reply to one of my letters. What else is there to aspire to in life?

A friend of mine (I'm calling her Patricia to protect her identity and also because I know it'll really annoy her) used the Subject Access Request with great finesse after finishing work at a high-street clothes retailer, following a number of altercations with her boss. She was not fond of her boss and it would be fair to say her boss was not fond of her. In fact, Patricia once described the boss to me as 'like a drowned rat if she had drowned in an open sewer and she wasn't a rat but Joseph Stalin'. Her reasons for not liking her seemed pure – she was rude and snappy, refused toilet breaks, belittled Patricia in front of customers, messed with her payments and gave her a useless reference that she couldn't give to other employers without looking like a Disney villain. She also monitored all the staff from her office using the CCTV, like watching a really weird and boring episode of *Big Brother*.

I was particularly cross with this woman because of the

reference – if you knew Patricia, you'd know she is the kindest, most considerate person you are ever likely to meet. So, in the pub Patricia and I hatched a plan to get revenge. I told her to make a Subject Access Request for some documents, just to scare the boss and also waste her time.

Patricia had a better idea. She made a formal request for the CCTV footage. Not any footage, just the footage including her, and between two specific times on a specific day. Remember, anyone who has filmed you legally has to present you with that footage if you make a request for it. Think of how many companies you could annoy doing that? I almost orgasm thinking about it.

What the boss didn't know was that the times Patricia had requested were completely arbitrary – she merely looked in her diary and found a day when she had definitely been working – but the effect on the boss was extraordinary. She sent the request email with me in the pub and the next morning received the following email. Names changed again for the usual boring legal reasons (omg I just fell asleep writing that sentence):

Patricia,
I need to ask, why do you want this information? I've watched the footage and there doesn't seem to be anything untoward happening. You are on the far right till and I am next to you for a short while doing some paperwork. You don't serve a customer. If there's an issue you want to raise, I'd prefer you did it with me transparently.
Thanks,
Susanne
General Manager

Patricia sent me the above, looking for guidance. Susanne is clearly absolutely shitting herself and still seems to think that she is Patricia's boss. Soz Susanne, you're just another snotty store manager to us now and we intend to ruin you. I drafted the below for her.

Hello Susanne,
    Legally, I am under no obligation to provide you with reasons for requesting the information and failure to do so will put you in contempt of the law. Please now respond to my request without delay. Don't worry, you will soon discover exactly why I have requested this.
    Regards,
    Patricia

She received a CD-ROM in the post about a week later with some completely innocuous footage of her standing looking bored at the till. She did nothing with it. She didn't even tell Susanne that she'd received it. About a month later Susanne emailed again, this time considerably breezier.

Hey Patricia,
    Just checking you received the CD with the requested information on it? Just checking, as I hadn't heard anything!
    Hope you're well!
    Susanne

Patricia devised the below herself and for this I think she is my finest student. She will go far. Perhaps she will write a book herself one day. If she does, I thoroughly recommend you read it.

Hello Susanne,
I have received the CD and passed it on to the relevant authorities.
Regards,
Patricia

That's probably the most beautiful email ever written. Well done Patricia, I am so, so proud of you.

One group of institutions that are famously slow to respond to these requests, and to pretty much any request for anything, is local councils. If I had a pound for every time I had to badger a local council I would have £13. They can hand out a parking fine as fast as it takes to affix it to your windscreen but anything meaningful takes an arduous stretch of time. They're like Venus flytraps, in that they don't do anything for ages and then eat an insect for nutrition when you originally asked them about bins.

I had an altercation with one council (guess what?! they can't be named legally!), who captured me driving in a bus lane and whacked me with a substantial fine. I've since been informed that the camera that got me is one of the highest-grossing traffic cameras in the UK. They're pulling in MILLIONS. I would argue if you're generating millions from one camera, there's something wrong with your road markings.

I approached with my usual request for any and all information they had on me and they played me at my own game. They bamboozled me with their own requests, claiming they needed additional information to access my data. They demanded I send them a £10 cheque (perfectly within their rights) and also specify from between which dates and from which departments I wanted the information. I explained:

'I am not sure which departments you have as a council but based on my work with other councils I have predicted which ones may have information and would like to request all data you have on me in the following departments: CCTV, traffic management, parking, medical, romantic, space, afterlife, ethereal and waste disposal. I'd like this information from between 9:14p.m. on 5 July 1988 (the time of my birth) and 7:32a.m. 6 June 2086 (the time of my death, approx.).'

They ignored this email – an unforgivable gesture, as they are legally obliged to respond to it. I waited a reasonable amount of time and emailed them again, including the following sentence:

'May I remind you that you are a governmental institution, and thus have powers when emails are ignored to hand out additional fines or take legal action. I am an individual, and thus have diminished powers and am reduced to sending irritating emails like this. However, I will be judged merely by your human laws whereas you will be judged at the gates of hell.'

They replied to apologise for the delay, which was due to a clerical error, and to tell me they had rejected my request for information because they didn't have an 'ethereal department' and that the fine had doubled. Wankers.

My most successful and high-profile use of a Subject Access Request came in the North. I arrived typically late for a stand-up performance and accidentally parked in a taxi rank – the sign was tiny, it was dark and I was rushed. Predictably, I received a £30 fine from the council and thus submitted a formal Subject Access Request to waste their time. In response, I received an email from some absolute jobsknob called Steph.

Mr Lycett,

I have passed your email on to the freedom of information team – hopefully they will be in touch with you soon.

Steph

Firstly, I expect this council's 'information team' means 'one person' and therefore I can say I've had sex with a 'team' of people. Her hyperbole aside, my main issue here is the use of the word 'hopefully'. It's infuriatingly vague. I went back to bloody Steph.

Steph,

Sadly 'hopefully' doth butter no parsnips.

Can I have an email for the person you've contacted at the FOI 'team'. My lawyers would like to contact them directly.

You have been very helpful and hopefully you won't get caught up in the forthcoming.

Joe Lycett

'Hopefully doth butter no parsnips' is an old Victorian phrase I'm trying to get back trending into use. I expect the hashtag would be #butterparsnips or something.

Worth noting here that when I refer to 'my lawyers', I am referring to people who do not exist. Also 'the forthcoming' is a vague threat designed to mean absolutely anything. It could mean I'm about to glass the woman. Steph responded:

> Mr Lycett,
>   I'm not sure what you mean about buttered parsnips. I have cc'ed the FOI team, who will advise.
> Steph

Then I got an email from someone called Colin, who I imagine was wanking as he wrote this:

Mr Lycett,
    Your request is very broad and so I have assumed you only want information pertinent to your recent parking fine. Attached is the evidence we have, which is a photograph of your car clearly parked in a taxi rank.
    Please let me know if you require any further information.
Sincerely,
Colin
FOI team

I imagine Colin was so pleased with himself that he ejaculated as he wrote the word 'pertinent'.

Colin,

   When you 'assume' you make an 'ass' out of 'u' and 'me'.

   I see that your evidence is nothing more than a picture of the words 'taxi rank' written on my car. I would argue this evidence is insufficient.

   Regards,

   Joe Lycett

P.S. Apologies for the delay in replying to your previous email – I was on the Costa del Sol. I have provided evidence of this.

My evidence was literally a picture I took in bed in Birmingham.

Mr Lycett,
   In order to reverse the fine you will need to provide evidence that you were NOT in a taxi rank.
Colin

Legally this is absolute nonsense, but whatever, I went back to Colin.

Colin,
   Evidence supplied, I was actually on the moon, as you can see clearly here.
Joe Lycett

I made this evidence on an app on my phone in ten seconds.

Mr Lycett,
   I have cancelled the fine.
Sincerely,
Colin

ADDENDUM

Months later, I had the good fortune of returning to the scene of this crime whilst on tour with my show, *That's The Way A-Ha A-Ha Joe Lycett* (I'm not joking, it was actually called that and I agree it is the best show title anyone has ever written). After the show, I arranged for the audience to join me in a short walk to the exact spot where I had received the fine – my car was there waiting. We took a lovely photo, which I forwarded to Colin.

Sorry Colin, I've done it again . . .
   Joe

No reply.

HOW TO DEAL WITH ESTATE AGENTS

Everyone hates estate agents. Even estate agents hate estate agents. It's not 'accessible' – it's a bungalow. It doesn't 'have character' – it has damp. It's not 'open-plan communal living' – it's a prison.

I've frequently had my time wasted by someone who has promised me the world and shown me a crack den. They're vultures of the worst kind, feasting on your hopes and dreams. Which is why I grasp any opportunity to annoy them with both hands and hold it aloft in my spacious, south-facing, open-plan living room.

I had the misfortune of dealing with one recently who insisted on saying things like, 'There's a Stannah stairlift but you could easily remove it' and 'The previous owner installed a system to lower them into the bath, of course you won't need that.' What an appalling thing to say to me. Yes, actually, I do need a machine to lower me into the bath – don't assume because I am a largely healthy young man that I am not incredibly lazy. A stairlift is an essential requirement for me, thank you very much.

An opportunity to irritate an estate agent arose in unusual circumstances when I stumbled across one based in London called Cluttons. During a trip to the capital (I was staying with friends in their *BEAUTIFULLY PRESENTED* two bedroom flat with great transport links), I spotted some adverts for their services on the tube, which comprised of stylish photographs of people in suits looking really professional and happy, even though it is impossible for them to be happy because they are estate agents. The name was emblazoned across the advert: CLUTTONS.

I'm sure they are very competent and accomplished – that is not in dispute and not my issue. My issue is that their name is 'Cluttons'. Saying it out loud produces an uncomfortable feeling, like when someone says 'moist' or 'tax return' or 'Amanda Holden'. It sounds rude. I'm guessing it's someone's name and I bet that person was, quite rightly, bullied for it.

Perhaps that's why Mr Cluttons became an estate agent. He felt belittled by his own name, so ultimately used it to belittle us all and ruin our chances of a reasonable abode for less than £800 a month. Now he has the power, but I have Twitter. So I devised a fun little game where I would post a rude sentence replacing the rudest word in the sentence with their Twitter name: '@cluttons'. I sat down at my laptop in the kitchen of my parents' *STUNNING* three bedroom period house and began to tweet . . .

Can anyone recommend a good shaving foam
that won't irritate my @cluttons?

Went for a bike ride and now I've chafed
my @cluttons.

Say what you like about Katie Price, you can't
deny she has fantastic @cluttons.

Maybe she's born with it. Maybe it's an
abnormal growth on her @cluttons.

Just heard I got a promotion at work and my
@cluttons swelled with joy.

If there's one thing I've learnt from my years of being on Twitter it's that tweeters love something silly, and as such Twitter became awash with @cluttons-based wordplay.

My beautiful Twitter followers, armed with a new word, began tweeting all number of saucy sentences at the Cluttons account:

@finchypoos
Oh god. Has anyone got any wet wipes?
Grandma's @cluttons are stuck together again.

@AidanJohnButler
my mom moans because I use my socks
to wipe up my @cluttons, it makes them hard to wash.

@BarleyCheech
I had a wasp dangerously close to my
@cluttons this morning.

@YellowNextDoor
When I broke my arm my mum had to help me
wash my @cluttons.

@BakersTweets
I played tennis the other day, wearing boxers
as I'd forgotten my briefs. As I lunged for a
forehand one of my @cluttons fell out.

@SamPicone
Apparently during the war they used to exchange
food for sexual favours, they called it Muttons for
@cluttons.

I went to bed (in my well-presented but poorly maintained bedroom, with inadequate storage and a slightly sinister smell) feeling smug. I imagined the next morning Mr Cluttons would wake (in his LUXURY converted loft apartment) to the barrage and be confused and hurt. Perhaps he would close the company. Maybe renovate an old wind farm. He could marry a poor, widowed refugee and adopt her children.

NO. He did none of those things.

I woke to a furious email from Twitter explaining that I had broken their code of conduct by encouraging other members to send 'spam tweets', and that if I didn't delete my previous posts and cease to post them then I would be BANNED from Twitter. I disagreed that I had encouraged such behaviour – I had merely illustrated to my fellow tweeters that this might be an enjoyable pastime – but, as devoted to the cause of annoying an estate agent as I am, I decided my Twitter account was too valuable to be sacrificed. I conceded and deleted the posts.

However, in my reply to Twitter I did use the sentence 'Don't get your Cluttons in a twist', which I was pretty thrilled about.

My relationship with the company is still strained and to this day, should I wish to read the tweets of Cluttons, I find a message informing me that I am blocked from following them or viewing their tweets.

Fortunately for me, I have no plans to use a London-based estate agent because I live in Birmingham and want to stay there. And if I was buying a property in London, the least of my worries would be that I was blocked by an estate agent on Twitter and more the fact that anyone who isn't a Russian billionaire or a member of One Direction is priced out to Watford.

Suck on my Cluttons, London.

Cluttons
@Cluttons

You are blocked from following @Cluttons and viewing @Cluttons's Tweets. Learn more

HOW TO RESPOND TO MORE HATE MAIL

I think it's important to reiterate what I put in my initial chapter on hate mail. Let me emphasise the key point: **DO NOT REPLY**. I cannot articulate more clearly how important that is.

I was the lucky recipient of this glorious bit of bile on the occasion of my first regular television appearance, a well-meaning game show on prime-time BBC called *Epic Win*. Hosted by Alexander Armstrong, the show encouraged ordinary people to demonstrate an incredible talent, to be judged by a celebrity panel. By 'incredible talent', I don't mean the sort of thing that would impress Simon Cowell but something sort of remarkable if you have been living in an isolation tank for thirty years. For example, one of the games consisted of a middle-aged fishmonger blindfolded and slapped in the face with various fish, which he would then identify merely by the sensations he felt as the scales brushed his face. It wasn't renewed for a second series. It was good experience.

After the first show aired, I remembered I had naively left my personal email address on my website. I presumed my inbox would now be flooded with fan emails, love letters and polite requests to see my genitals. Instead, there was just one email.

From: *NICKY*
To: *Joe Lycett*
Subject: *Please, Motherfucker*

My TV licence is up for renewal in 13 days. I'm not paying it.

I won't have my hard worked money go to pay you, unfunny twat, and the even worse and more annoying joke stealer dogger utter cunt Manford.

Fuck off! Fucking terrible! I'm going to find out who your dad is!

You are not on TV because of your talent, you don't have any. Fucking right wing cunt! A comic for the David Cameron age.

Stick your posh voice back up your horse faced mother's cunt.

Fuck off now and join Daddy's firm. Fucking prick. Please.

X

1–0 to Nicky. I like that he says 'please' at the end, like it's a polite request and I LOVE that he put a kiss at the end. Perhaps it was deliberate, more likely force of habit. The 'Manford' he refers to is comedian Jason Manford, who also appeared on *Epic Win* and has since rejected my suggestion of using 'annoying joke stealer dogger utter cunt' as his Twitter bio.

Also, he is presuming that, as I have a posh voice (up for debate, I pronounce 'tooth' as 'tuth'), I must be a right-wing Cameron supporter. He clearly dislikes right-wingers and from that we can deduce that he must be left-leaning. It made me think, 'Who do I know called Nick or Nicky who is left-leaning?'

I replied:

From: Joe Lycett
To: NICKY
Subject: Re: Please, Motherfucker

Dear Nick Clegg,
Thank you for your request to book my act, in which I stick my posh voice back up my horse faced mother's cunt. I've spoken to Mother – she is delighted, as we've not had many bookings recently and she wants to buy an AGA.
Please can you suggest some dates?
Kind Regards,
Joe 'Motherfucker' Lycett
xxx

1–1. I made sure to put three kisses to demonstrate that I am in love with him.

From: NICKY

Please fuck off cunt. I'm reporting you to
Channel 4. You prick.

No kiss on this reply, I had obviously upset him. 2–1 to me. As much as I'm sure Channel 4 would've loved the feedback, the show was broadcast on the BBC.

From: Joe Lycett

Dearest Nick Clegg,
    Thank you for the swift reply but you didn't mention a date for us to perform. How about Boxing Day? That's my day off from the orphanage for sick and starving children.
Yours eternally,
Joe 'Motherfucker' Lycett
xxxxxxx

P.S. Do you have wheelchair access?

I don't know why I added the postscript on this one, but I made myself laugh with it. 3–1.

From: NICKY

Please leave me alone.

From: Joe Lycett

My Darling Nick Clegg,
	If you now need to cancel, we will need to charge a cancellation fee.
	Mother has already bought her costume. She spent hours online searching for the right style of arseless chaps. Her cluttons look fantastic.
All my love,
Joe 'Motherfucker' Lycett
xxxxxxxxxxxxxxxxxxxxxxxxxxxxxxx

Your move, Clegg.

From: NICKY

Boxing Day is fine.

4–1 and that's full time.

I KILLED TWO BIRDS WITH
ONE STONE, WHICH IS ULTIMATELY
WHY I LOST MY JOB AT
THE AVIARY.

HOW TO
WORK IN ADVERTISING

The Activia yoghurt adverts do my nut in. Their whole premise is basically, 'Eat a yoghurt with Gok Wan, have a laugh, have a nice shit.' I would appreciate it more if they were just honest and said, 'Our yoghurts are quite nice and might stop your arse from falling apart.'

The yoghurt itself is FINE. There are far nicer ones – I'll be honest, I still love a Petit Filou. I would happily snatch one from a toddler's feeble grasp. By 'I would', I mean 'I have'.

But the new adverts?! Vile. Whereas Martine McCutcheon had a dignified, almost distant tone, in the recent offerings Gok Wan appears in full mania mode. Surrounded by women laughing and smiling violently at each other, he screeches the benefits of Activia yoghurt before the women hold pictures of a smiling face over their abdomens. They have 'happy tummies', they tell us, arrogantly. No. If you could see the contents of your tummy, I don't think the first word you'd think of would be 'happy'. It would be 'ambulance'.

I was discussing this recently with a female friend, who mentioned that she had been emailed by a woman from the Activia team called Cynthia Finke (a name that sounds like I made it up when drunk) asking for help with their new ad campaign. They wanted women to explain why things were better for them on the outside when they felt good on the inside. OH I DON'T KNOW CYNTHIA, I JUST GENERALLY FEEL MUCH BETTER WHEN I'M NOT CLOSE TO SHITTING MYSELF.

My friend thought the email, as with a lot of their campaigns, was 'patronising'. The crux of the email was this simple request:

Just complete the following sentence:
'When I take care of myself from the inside out ...'

They were basically canvassing bored women to write their ads for them. This seemed like fun to me. Helpfully, they'd given some piss-poor examples of their own:

Digestive Health
When I take care of myself from the inside out,
I can focus on what's really important.

Wellbeing
When I take care of myself from the inside out,
it's sunny whatever the forecast.

Body
When I take care of myself from the inside out, every hour is for the taking.

What? 'Every hour is for the taking'? What does that even mean? I knew I could do better.

There was an email address to send your suggestions to and a request to send a picture. And, well, you know me. This was unmissable.

I logged into my email as Samantha Salamander, and got in touch right away.

Hi Cynthia,

   I just got your email about the Activia campaign and think it's just really super fun!

   I'm currently off work as a result of a serious and brutal motoring accident, so have had the time to think of a couple of ideas for taglines for your campaign. What about something like: 'Everybody hurts but not everybody YOGhurts!' I also noticed 'yoghurt' is an anagram for 'go for it' if you spell it 'go hur yt!' Sorry if they're not useful, I'm on a lot of painkillers!!!

   I've put some of my thoughts for the 'When I take care of myself from the inside out . . .' idea. I really hope some of them get used 'cause I just really love yoghurt!

   When I take care of myself from the inside out, every moment just feels really special to me. :)

When I take care of myself from the inside out, I realise there's no 'can't' in 'yoghurt'! :)

When I take care of myself from the inside out, I have the most fantastic sex (!) ;)

When I take care of myself from the inside out, I get so many things done in the days despite the constant voices telling me to kill. :)

When I take care of myself from the inside out, I just feel really fantastic and not lonely but still quite angry. :)

When I take care of myself from the inside out, I don't ruin everything for you like you say I do, Steve. :£

When I take care of myself from the inside out, I stop wanting to psychologically damage my family. :|

I've attached a recent picture of myself.

Thanks so much, please don't not reply!

Samantha

Samantha received no reply. If I'm honest, I was offended for Samantha that the people of Activia didn't take her suggestions seriously, as I would've happily seen any one of those additions at the very front of their campaign. Imagine how gripping the campaign would be with this tagline:

ACTIVIA
FEEL BETTER FROM THE INSIDE OUT AND SILENCE THE VOICES TELLING YOU TO KILL.

I suspected they possibly wanted a better role model for women, a high-achiever, a mover, a shaker, someone with power. I realised I knew exactly who that was: Angela Merkel.

Fresh from emailing Birmingham City Council about their Christmas markets (see the How to survive Christmas chapter), Angie turned her sights on Activia:

Guten Tag Frau Activia,

Ich has komst to mein attention dat you are looking for inspiration from powerful frauliens. Ich habe some thoughts for you and your campaign with ich thinke will be very helpful because ich am Chancellor of Deutscheland und das ist das best job in Europe. Bitte.

When ich tachen care auf meinself from das inside out, ich can run das EU sehr gut.

When ich tachen care auf meinself from das inside out, ich habe ein sehr gut gut.

When ich tachen care auf meinself from das inside out, ich feel better equipped to consider complex social expenditure issues which involve the whole of das EU creating a cohesive und comprehensive plan to support migrants from war-torn countries.

When ich tachen care auf meinself from das inside out, ich still love a bit of knob auf mein brot.

Ich hope you use mein suggestions, otherwise ich will destroy your company mit EU sanctions. Ich much prefer Petits Filous, even though there ist no spoon das fits auf das pot.

Auf wiedersehen,

Angie M

xoxo

P.S. May ich suggest some new flavours. Ich love kokosnuss (coconut), haselnuss (hazelnut), und mein favourite ist peanuss.

You're not going to believe this, but they didn't even reply to the Chancellor of Germany!

Despite my best efforts, and the efforts of the most powerful woman in Europe, it looks like we're destined for a life of being talked down to by people who make a fucking yoghurt.

HOW TO
SPEAK TO THE LIVING

A clairvoyant is a man or woman – but normally a middle-aged, lonely woman – who is convinced that they can speak to the dead, probably because their slightly haughty, patronising tone stopped people wanting to talk to them in real life about twenty-five years ago.

They are keen to say publicly that their techniques work, but avoid scientific examination by saying things like, 'Science can't explain everything' and 'Get that pipette and Petri dish away from me.'

Basically, they're full of shit.

I have many issues with the idea of ghosts, but the main one is that most people see them when they are already in a creepy situation. Ghost sightings, or 'feeling a presence', almost always begin with someone in a spooky environment, explaining that they felt vulnerable. It's late at night, or at the end of their bed, or they're in a forest, or they're round at Amanda Holden's house. Ghost stories almost never start mid-afternoon on a Tuesday in a well-lit branch of TK Maxx.

I once went to see a clairvoyant with some of my family 'cause I had the night off and I was curious. The woman said a few things like, 'You think about things a lot at night' (duh) and 'There's a guardian angel with you when you're on stage.' Well that guardian angel clearly had a night off when I played Stockton in 2008. Thanks for the confused silence, guys!

I'm not in the camp of people who think that psychics or clairvoyants are bare-faced liars though. I don't think they tell people they're speaking to their loved ones when actually they know it's all nonsense. I think what happens is that they have confused their subconscious monologue with people in the afterlife. If you think now about an elderly woman in front of you, your mind could easily conjure something plausible for her to say. Perhaps she's whispering, 'I still love you' or 'I forgive you' or 'I know you have an erection under there.' Sorry if you are reading this in a creepy place and now you think there's a ghost with you. I'm not sorry if you're getting turned on by an imaginary old woman.

So in the spirit of channelling your subconscious, I wrote to one clairvoyant, called Frances, doing just that. I found her details on a flyer in a pub in Birmingham, which included the following offer:

> FREE FIRST TIME SPIRIT READING OVER SMS TEXT!!!

Well I'm not one to turn down a free offer am I?! I contacted Frances to try and speak to my mother, Helen. My mother, Helen, is alive and well.

> Hello Frances, I'm trying to contact someone. Can you help???

> Yes. First reading is free! What is your name and who are you trying to contact?

> My name is Joe and I'm trying to contact my mother, Helen.

> Do you have anything of hers to hand?

> Yes, I have a scarf.

> OK, hold the scarf in your hand and text me the first three words that come to mind. It can be anything, don't try and edit yourself.

> Casserole. Ford Focus. Abusive.

> OK, I'm getting something.

> There's something to do with glasses?

> It could be a pair of glasses or something made of glass. Does that make sense?

> Yes.

> She's got a problem with the glasses. Is there anything that might link to?

She wears glasses?

She's saying she's sorry.

OK, what about?

She's just saying, 'There's so much. Sorry about the mess.'

OK, that's fine. Does she say where she is?

I'm not sure but she's happy where she is. She's smiling.

Oh well that's good for her. Does she know when she's going to be back?

I'm losing contact. She says she'll see you soon and she'll make it up to you about the glass.

Oh I see, is she saying for me to smash the glass?

I'm not sure. I've lost contact.

OK, I'm going to smash the glass.

What glass? I don't think she wants you to put yourself in danger.

Well I'm outside the house without my keys, so I'm going to have to get in somehow.

???

Oh she just got back, it's OK.

She just got back? Is she in the spirit world?

What? No, of course not. She went to the garden centre.

Please don't contact me again.

OK, sure. Everything you said was true though. She was happy. She loves the garden centre.

HOW TO

CLAIM FOR AN ACCIDENT THAT WASN'T YOUR FAULT

I think it was the great William Wordsworth who pronounced: 'Where there's blame, there's a claim.' It might not've been him, I've not checked. But it is a quote that has stood the test of time and is no truer than today. You can sue anyone for pretty much anything. You will probably have encountered adverts encouraging you to sue someone because you slipped over and you don't want to accept that it's a natural hazard when you work in a lube shop.

There are now established law firms dealing exclusively with these cases. Like many aspects of law, I've always thought making your living suing people for simple, blameless accidents to be peculiar. You might argue that I can't talk, I've made a career out of being annoying over email, but at least I don't claim to be respectable for it. On the other hand, these men and women are certified lawyers who have studied for years, learning all sorts of amazing and, complex philosophical things about accountability and justice in Old English guff, just so that they can get £300 for a blind woman who tried to climb a ladder wearing bamboo stilts.

I wondered what would happen if you had an accident whilst working at the law firm that specialises in suing for accidents. Could you sue yourself? Or would you just have to accept that accidents happen and that is just part of life? Probably.

Then, as if sent from on high, I found myself choking on a grape whilst laughing at an advert for one of these law firms, so I decided to see if I could claim compensation for this.

One of my weirder emails, this:

To Whom It May Concern,

I am writing to you, as I wish to claim compensation for an accident that wasn't my fault. Let me explain very clearly: IT WAS YOUR FAULT.

It was a crisp, spring morning in February and I had just settled down in my work chair to check my emails. My premises are a small and humble office in Telford, and I am PA to the owner of a business selling gluten-free crumpets. My boss is generous and thoughtful, and always ensures that there is fruit available to us to boost our energy and immune systems.

I heard a voiceover on the television that asked, 'Have you had an accident that wasn't your fault?' I swivelled my chair towards the television to watch, as I consider one of life's great pleasures to be the low production values of these adverts. This particular promotion was for your firm and involved a woman slipping over and damaging her leg. She received thousands of pounds in compensation and I am absolutely thrilled for her. But I was too distracted to hear about this problem in any detail as I was CHOKING NEARLY TO DEATH.

The reason for my predicament is that as the woman in the advert fell, I observed her neck, and it made me laugh. Her neck was hilarious. The woman could be fairly described as 'ripe' – a rotund and juicy specimen, perfectly pretty, but clearly not unfamiliar with butter. I'm not judging her, I love a bit of butter myself. But as the woman fell, her neck moved independently of her, as if it was its own separate organism, barely attached, and as it flicked from one side to the other, it appeared to increase the speed of propulsion throwing her to the ground. My laugh at this image was so involuntary, so unexpected, that the grape I was eating got lodged in my trachea, and I began to violently cough.

In the moment, I found the idea that I was choking merely because I was laughing at a woman's neck hysterically funny in itself, and that made me laugh more and, as I laughed and choked, the grape got lodged further still. It became a cyclical process of laughter, choking, imagining my obituary reading 'Died whilst laughing at a fat neck', then laughing more, then choking again. The hysteria only subsided when my boss thumped me on the back and the grape was propelled from my throat and onto a nearby gluten-free crumpet.

I haven't been able to speak since my injuries, not to mention the trauma, and have been forced to take a week off work. I demand compensation.

Thank you for your time.

Johnny Norris

You guessed it: no reply.

HOW TO BE AN ONLINE ACTIVIST

I am an activist. I know this because I sign fifty petitions a day. Who doesn't love a petition? There's one for everything: 'Stop tax cuts', 'Ban fox hunting', 'Pay doctors more', 'Get Joe Lycett off my television.' It's an easy and convenient way of showing all of society that I can spell my name, that I know my postcode and that I have an opinion that I sort of care about but not really.

The are a million petition websites but my favourite has to be the official government one, called the Parliamentary Petitions website, which is designed to make the Great British Public feel like they are being listened to whilst simultaneously not listening to them at all. Anyone can set up a petition as long as they have a UK postcode, which is unlucky if you're homeless and want to set up a 'More rights for the homeless' petition. In the terms and conditions on the website, there are some vague promises and pretend numbers, such as '10,000 signatures means we will have a look at it in our lunch break' and '100,000 signatures means we will consider doing something about it and then get distracted by Netflix' and '1 million signatures means we will be really impressed and talk about your petition in the corridor before smashing it into the bin with the power of twenty men.'

This is not the first time the government have set up a completely pointless website. I remember when the Conversative/ Liberal Democrat coalition first emerged, there was a website established where anyone could suggest ways for the government to reduce public spending. They spent a load of money setting up the website and most of the entries were things like 'Stop immigrants coming in' and 'Pay civil servants less.' What fantastic, insightful, realistic solutions!

I trolled this particular website by simply posting recipes that required cheap ingredients. Amidst the suggestions of reducing MPs' wages and spending less on the BBC, you would find posts from me that included 'Apple, pear and cherry compote' and 'Beef and vegetable casserole'. I'll never be sure but I bet some people in Parliament had a go at my 'Chicken and white bean stew'. I can confirm it is completely delicious and freezable, shaving valuable minutes from the day queuing at the Parliament canteen that can then be used reading more petitions!

The official promise on the petitions website is that they will 'consider debating it in Parliament' if a petition gets over 100,000 signatures. I'm not mad on the phrase 'consider debating' – it's a bit like saying, 'I will think about thinking about it.' It means nothing. It butters no parsnips.

Here is a list of petitions that have received over the 100,000-signature threshold according to the government petition website as of summer 2016.

Block Donald J. Trump from UK entry (581,862 signatures)

Stop all immigration and close the UK borders until ISIS is defeated (463,498 signatures)

Accept more asylum seekers and increase support for refugee migrants in the UK (450, 286 signatures)

Also, a notable entry for 'closest to getting to the threshold and not quite making it' is this one:

Don't kill our bees! Immediately halt the use of neonicotinoids on our crops (99,908 signatures)

Sorry bees, but just not quite enough people give a shit.

You will notice, nothing has been done about any of the above. Donald Trump is not blocked, immigration still continues and we haven't accepted more asylum seekers. Whatever your personal beliefs on these issues, observing that they've all had half a million signatures and nothing done about them might make you think that the petitions website is a complete waste of time – and you'd be right!

My attention was drawn to the Parliamentary Petitions website initially by a petition for a vote of no confidence in Jeremy Hunt. I'd never signed a petition before but when I saw one against Jeremy Hunt, I couldn't resist. If you're not familiar with him, imagine one of the vampires from *Buffy*, only 100 times less compassionate and in control of the NHS. I signed the petition, along with hundreds of thousands of others. The official response: 'The House of Commons Petitions Committee has decided not to schedule a debate on this petition.' What a surprise.

In my frustration, I set up my own petition:

Vote of no confidence in this website.

My blurb was simple:

> *115,000 people signed a petition for a vote of no confidence in Jeremy Hunt and you did jack all about it so I propose another vote of no confidence in this website and the weak-willed, grey-suited end of bells who run it.*

I was surprised to discover a few hours later that they had rejected my petition (it had already received ten signatures!) on the grounds that it is 'not clear what the petition is asking us to do'. I think it's very clear. I'm asking you to close your own website. Perhaps they weren't sure what 'end of bells' means? It's a Ye Olde English phrase for 'Member of Parliament'.

I decided if they weren't going to take me seriously, I wasn't going to take them seriously either, so I set up a final petition, which was literally just the smiling pile of poo emoji.

The title:

And the blurb for this one even simpler:

Again I was rejected on the grounds that my petition was 'nonsense'. I would argue that spending considerable reserves of government money on opening a petitions website that gets hundreds of thousands of signatures and then does nothing about any of them is probably more nonsensical. Very much the pot calling the kettle nonsense.

As a result of being a double-rejectee from the petitions website, I had the great pleasure of being listed on their 'rejected petitions' section. Looking through it has since become one of my favourite pastimes. Here are some genuine rejectees from the Parliamentary Petitions website:

Build an ice rink in Southampton.

I love the idea that there was a big town meeting in Southampton where all the residents said they wanted an ice rink and someone said, 'I will sort this', before realising they had no idea how to make it happen other than writing it on a petitions website.

Amend the way cats are undervalued in today's society and enforce current laws.

I'm not precisely sure how we undervalue cats – if anything, I feel undervalued by my cat. I am nothing more than a reluctant source of Dreamies and head scratching. She gives me no consideration for actually being fucking allergic.

Tell your mum that you love her.

Maybe just tell your mum and not the Internet?

Bring back Smarties McFlurry.

To be fair, I agree with this 100 per cent.

This is just the tip of a pointless iceberg. The poor folks running the site must have to trawl through this shit every day – no wonder when something actually worth voting for gets posted it gets largely ignored. As the saying goes: no man can be productive if he has to politely decline building an ice rink in Southampton.

Not long after my poo petition had been rejected, it came to my attention that anyone who had signed it had received an email telling them why it had been rejected, which included my personal email address. I think the technical team presumed that you'd just forward the petition on to people from your own email account so it wouldn't matter, but I had chosen to post the link on my Facebook page, which meant a load of people who I might not necessarily want my private email to be shared with now had it. My address could fall into the hands of someone who, I don't know, likes to send silly spam emails? And people who send silly spam emails are the worst.

Naturally, this is a breach of data protection, a breach by Her Majesty's Government no less, and a complaint to them would have to warrant a reply. I started pretty dry:

To Whom It May Concern,

I had a petition rejected today which, whilst I disagree with the decision, I accept.

However, it has come to my attention that some of those who signed the petition have received an email that includes the private email address I used to start it. It states very clearly on your form that you use only the name, and 'We won't publish your personal details anywhere or use them for anything other than this petition.' You have not kept this promise.

This is a serious breach of security on your part and I am looking into this as a legal matter.

Regards,

Joe Lycett

There was a bit of fannying around after this, involving an email from someone called Anne-Marie who said the technical team would be 'in touch soon'. Spare me your fucking vagaries, Anne.

Then John Johnson, fake name, who according to Twitter invented the petitions website, contacted me himself. What an honour!

Dear Joe Lycett,

Thanks for bringing this to our attention.

Surely your petition supporters know your email address from when you forwarded our email to them, to ask for support?

However, I can see that you might have used a different address to forward on our email. I'll look into getting this changed.

John

--

John Johnson
Product Manager

John is a product manager who doesn't know his own product. Just because the link to sign the petition was sent to me in an email doesn't mean that I forwarded it on via email. A link can be spread in a multitude of ways. I illustrated this to him as clearly as I could . . .

Hello John,

Thank you for getting back to me on this.

Once I had set up the petition I decided, rather than taking the obvious route of sharing it with friends over email, that this issue was simply too important and would demand me to be more creative. I began the painstaking task of crocheting the petition details and URL into fifteen individual flannels, each with their own unique design and illustrations. I spent hours preparing them and I consider them to be amongst some of my life's finest work.

Armed with my 'petition flannels', I took to the streets of London screeching, 'Hear ye, hear ye! Getchar 'tition flannels 'ere! Only 'ere can ye find the link to tell them up in government 'bout this most heinous of issues!' As you can imagine, there was much interest and concern. I handed out the flannels to those who I thought would appreciate my message, all of them complete strangers, who now have my personal email address and are barraging me with requests for more of my crochet work.

Regardless, I am still disappointed that your website deems my petition consisting only of smiling piles of poo emojis to be 'nonsense'.

Many thanks,

Joe Lycett

To date I have received no reply but then he may be crocheting his response into a flannel and that takes time, believe me.

To conclude, you may well want to sign a petition in the future and there's nothing wrong with that. But it could well lead to hassle and it's worth lowering your expectations. Lower them again. Are they in the gutter? Lower them further.

Petitions are a vanity project. If you want an ice rink in Southampton, I'm really sorry, but you're going to have to build it yourself.

I CAN COMPLETE A RUBIK'S
CUBE IN 20 SECONDS...

...IF BY 'COMPLETE A RUBIK'S
CUBE' YOU MEAN 'POUR
A GLASS OF RIOJA AND
LOOK OUT OF THE WINDOW'.

HOW TO
BE A FOOTBALL FAN

I have recently become a fan of West Bromwich Albion football club because my friend Karen told me to – she said that they are 'the best team'. I have since discovered that describing West Brom as 'the best team' is like saying sex with me makes people 'feel largely satisfied'. It is simply statistically inaccurate.

I have been to a couple of games at the stadium now, but before that I decided to watch one in an old man pub in a rough suburb of Birmingham with a name something like The Puke and Vomit. The woman behind the bar could only be described as looking like a dessicated scrotum. She didn't like me because I ordered a white wine spritzer – I will never forget the way she peered into my eyes, furious, before asking, 'What the fook's that?' Terrified, I explained to her that a white wine spritzer is a delicious and simple mix of soda water and white wine. She disappeared behind the bar for a worrying amount of time before emerging with a pint of soda water and a full bottle of dessert wine. I asked how much this would cost me. 'I don't know, a fiver?' It was the best night of my life. I love the football. Although I did get some disapproving looks at one point when I meant to shout, 'Come on, lads' but ended up saying, 'Come on the lads.'

Peculiarly, I have not yet come across an existing book that can help novices learn how to become football fans – this is probably because I have not looked. Plus when you turn up to a match, I don't think there is a pamphlet explaining the rules and regulations – there might be, but I've been to two matches. Well, one and a half, I got bored at the second one. If you are not accustomed to the game, you are somehow expected to simply pick it up. This would be acceptable if it weren't the case that fandom is complicated and fraught with danger. Through my thorough research of attending one and a half games and occasionally checking the scores on an app, I have drawn up a list of tips that might help you on your path to becoming a true football fan.

Here are the tips. Get ready for the tips. Show us your tips.

SHOUT JOB ADVICE TO STRANGERS
The linesman (who has trained for two decades and has sacrificed countless opportunities to spend time with his children by being at football matches every weekend) doesn't know a fucking thing and is a fucking prick and you should tell him that now. Loudly.

REFERENCE PEOPLE'S SALARIES
In normal life it is uncouth to mention how much people are earning or use it as a bludgeon against them, but in football this

is not the case and is considered a perfectly acceptable way to behave. In fact, I can think of no better way to express my disgust at the performance of a football player who has consistently demonstrated a skill and dedication for the sport that eclipses any achievements I have ever or will ever make. For example, if a player has scored lots of goals over their career but they're feeling a little under the weather during one match and miss a goal, I will shout, '£30,000 a week?! Waste of every penny.' I now do this in other walks of life and will bark '£7.20 an hour?!' when my Subway sandwich doesn't have enough gherkin.

CLENCH YOUR FISTS

It is important to show that you are angry and serious about the game. By clenching your fists, others will know you care. If someone gets within your personal space you may consider punching them to the ground.

DRESS TO IMPRESS

You will need to add some sensational new outfits to your wardrobe in order to fit in with your fellow supporters. It's time to invest in a Football Shirt. It may sound odd, but this is the same shirt as worn by the players on the pitch – I thought that this would confuse people in the stands into thinking that I was a player who had a day off and was watching from the crowd, but apparently this is standard practice. You can also get scarves, hats, shorts, shoes, wristbands and teddy bears. The most devoted fans are the ones who wear all of the merchandise at once.

CHANT POETRY

I have noticed that some fans will chant short poems, which others will then repeat. One of them will start, then the others will join in gradually until a crescendo of shared human voices emerges, telling the goalkeeper he's a 'tiny hunded fucking twat'. (You can achieve a similar shared human experience by masturbating on group chat rooms late at night.) There are many different football chants you can engage in and you can write your own! You may be creatively inclined yourself, but if you are not you could bring along a copy of Keats's 'Ode on a Grecian Urn' to aggressively hiss into someone's face. Alternatively, take this book with you, as I have written some short chants that you are welcome to use when you are next a la football:

I don't know but I'll take a guess,
the other team are an absolute mess.

I don't know but it's been said,
one day we will all be dead.

I don't know but I'm sure I'm right,
if you disagree let's have a fight.

I don't know but I think it's true,
the other team smell like poo.

I don't know but I've been told,
football players can't grow old.

I don't know but I'll take a punt,
the referee is a fucking . . . nice guy.

NB: After each of these, you are expected to clap. This is the standard clap formation:

CLAP. CLAP. CLAP-CLAP-CLAP. CLAP-CLAP-CLAP-CLAP. CLAP-CLAP.

NB: You can chant individual words after these clap formations such as, 'football', 'goalie', 'ball', 'despair', 'Jesus', 'pineapple', 'denouement' or 'Debbie'.

SOME KEY TERMS

As with any sport, football utilises an intimidating amount of jargon. Learn the following off by heart and you are sure to impress any football fans you encounter with your extensive knowledge of the sport's key terms.

Offside
This is a term used to refer to a player who has taken the ball to the wrong side of the pitch. This can happen when the player feels he has been belittled by his teammates because they didn't compliment him on his shoes, and so he makes a stand and takes the ball 'offside'.

Not involved in play
Used to describe literally everyone in the world who is not playing in the football match you are watching. For example, you might say, 'I am enjoying watching this Leicester vs Tottenham game, even though my mother is not involved in play.'

Half-time
What some idiots call 'the interval'. This is an opportunity for the audience to discuss who their favourite player is and smash a rival fan in the face with a gin and tonic.

4–4–2
These are the first three digits of David Beckham's PIN.

Cruyff turn
Misspelling of 'crap turn'. A crap turn is when a player who dreams of being in showbusiness does a crap variety act in the interval.

Fergie time
This is a rare break in play where all the players sit in the dressing room and look at pictures of Fergie from The Black Eyed Peas to

calm their nerves whilst listening to her track 'Big Girls Don't Cry' on repeat. Not to be mistaken with 'will.i.am time', which is used to get the players fired up.

Golden goal

Many football clubs are owned by international billionaires and some will make their goals out of gold to demonstrate their considerable wealth. Annoyingly, due to regulations, you will never know which goals are golden because they all have to be painted white.

Keepie uppie

A phrase used by WAGs (wives and girlfriends) when engaging in post-match drunken coitus.

Lost the dressing room

This is used when the manager of a team has a lot on his mind and can't find the dressing room.

Nutmeg

A fragrant spice that some football players enjoy sprinkled on their morning latte.

Square ball

A practical joke played by some referees where a square football will be introduced into play to see how long it takes for the teams to notice. There have been some instances where a whole team have failed to spot that the ball is square for an entire season.

Sudden death

This is a last resort used when all other ways of deciding the winning team have been exhausted. First there is extra time, then penalties, and then finally sudden death. The players wait in an office until one of them dies, thus crowning the other team as the winners.

Do your best

Good advice for anyone in any profession.

Wanker

Usually reserved for the referee when he makes a decision you profoundly disagree with.

There you have it; now you are a true football fan! Congratulations! Now it's time to get on down to a game and tell everyone you meet that you are more of a fan than they are. If they disagree, smash them in the face repeatedly until your fists are crushed.

HOW TO
COPE ON FACEBOOK

It is unfortunate but inevitable that any book discussing the trials and foibles of modern life will need to include a chapter on Facebook. Depending on who you ask, Mark Zuckerberg's brainchild has brought us closer together or pushed us much, much further apart. If anything, I feel estranged from my actual friends and much closer to Mark Zuckerberg. You never truly understand someone better than when you are subjected to their dreadful ideas. A separate app for messages, Mark? Sure! I have a separate folder in my contacts for you, labelled: Wankers.

But despite all the criticism, Facebook can be a fantastic tool for good, as long as it is used wisely. As my mother always says, 'With great social media platforms come great swathes of arseholes posting BuzzFeed articles and pictures of their dog.'

I use Facebook for its primary purpose, the reason it was invented in the first place: to show off about my life and make it look better than it is. It's important that all of your friends know how well everything is going, even though you're crying in the conservatory. Here's a classic example of the sort of post I'm on about:

Joe Lycett: What a fantastic year 2015 has been. I ran my first marathon, travelled to 23 different countries and earned my first million! My New Year's resolution is to stop being a compulsive liar. Thanks guys!!!

One common way of showing off on Facebook is to post about an upcoming trip, under the guise of 'asking for help'. Here's one from my friend Craig, who has a beard and works in a craft beer shop:

Craig: Any tips for New York? Going next week for first time.

Don't get me wrong, I'm happy for Craig – I wish him well and he's a nice guy, but I'm mainly incredibly bitter because I've never been to New York and I want to go, but I'm not allowed because I have to go and do a show in Stockton. I decided a sarcastic comment was the only way to respond:

Joe: Why not check out some of the great bars and restaurants?

Craig commented something about me being a 'sarcy twat' and made a point of tagging me in all his New York photos. You win this time Craig.

There was a time when I thought that accepting everyone who requested my friendship on Facebook was a good idea, the logic being that it would allow me to publicise my comedy shows to a wider audience and also that I would make a ton of great new interesting friends along the way. This was absolutely not the case and it didn't take long for the many peculiars and unusuals of life to find their way into my message inbox.

At its worst, I was receiving a minimum of one spam message a day, which I was largely ignoring. Highlights included a man offering to sell me bulk quantities of cheap trainers, a promise of sexual intercourse with a woman in Thailand if I sent her my full address and scan of my passport, and my personal favourite was the offer of a business partnership where I would import whisky into the country by going in 50/50 with a guy in Japan for the small buy-out fee of £26.

I've always been fascinated by this sort of attempt to extort money from people over the Internet; the hit rate must be dreadfully low but yet still substantial enough for it to be worth the while of the people trying it. I expect part of it is quite fun, and the excitement when someone responds to the bait must provide such an adrenaline rush. But it's also deeply immoral and callous, which I imagine makes it a niche sort of person who attempts it in the first place. One chap, Bill Roberts, contacted me fairly persistently, trying to offer me a substantial sum of money that he had procured from Mark Zuckerberg. He also loved a random CAPS LOCK. I'm not one to pass up an offer, and so after about five messages I replied.

NB: I don't know what Bill Roberts actually looks like but I imagine it's something like Conservative MP Eric Pickles.

Hi Joe,
    You are welcome. We have been looking for a way to get you because your name is among the lucky winner selected on Facebook for 10yrs anniversary. My name is Bill Roberts, I'm a special agent working with WORLD BANK and PRESIDENT OBAMA to give money donated by the founder of Facebook (Mark Zuckerberg).
    The money is from Mark Zuckerberg (founder of Facebook) for the 10YRS ANNIVERSARY. You can claim between $50,000.00 and $2,000,000.00 and I will like to know if you want your money in CASH or CHEQUE.
    I will be waiting soon
    Thanks
    SPECIAL AGENT Bill Roberts

Are you there Joe? We have been waiting for you. Congratulations!!!

Are you there now?

Oh yes sorry, I've been very busy refilling a 10ft deep hole I dug in my garden. I could only complete the work at night so it's taken longer than expected. Tell me about this money.

Yes I will tell you now.
We have been looking for a way to get you because your name is among the LUCKY WINNER selected on Facebook for 10yrs anniversary

My name is bill Roberts, I am a Special Agent from the International Monetary Fund (IMF). I am in charge of the money from Mark Zuckerberg (founder of Facebook) to the lucky people for the 10YRS ANNIVERSARY.

This is just fantastic news. I find it difficult to earn money because I have no hands.

Yes, this is like the Programme pension fund as BONUS for the new year.

I don't understand any of what you just said but this is still fantastic news. How much money do I get?

You can choose between £50,000.00 (Fifty Thousand Pounds) and £2,000,000.00 (Two Million Pounds) depends the amount you choose. Therefore, I will like to know if you want your money in CHEQUE or CASH?

That's tricky. Could I choose a different amount? And I'm not sure about CHEQUE or CASH do you have PAYPAL?

Paypal cannot take such large amount and we are delivering CASH or CHEQUE to be sure the right person gets the money
We will come and deliver the money in person so no worries.

OK well that makes perfect sense. I'll take it in CASH in a LEATHER BRIEFCASE .

Yes that is right because you won't have to wait any cheque to clear in the bank. Now I will need some details from you to confirm the deliver.

Of course I will give you all of my details, why wouldn't I.

Here are the info you will send to us now to claim your money.
Full name ......
Full Home Address ...
Date of birth ....
Married/single ....
E-mail ......
Facebook email ......
Cell / Txt number .....
What do you do for a living ....
Do you Own a house or Rent Apt .....
Have you lost money before ....
How much .....

We want to be sure we are giving the money to the right person. You have to be honest with us in giving the right information.
This details will enable us to deliver your money safely and will be use to identify you when delivering the money. I will be waiting for your mail soon. CONGRATULATION!!!!

OK here are my full details.
Full name: Philip, Prince
Full Address: Buckingham Palace, London, SW1A 1AA
Date of Birth: 10 June 1921
Married/single: It's complicated
Email: pppeterpppeterson@gmail.com
Tel (during working hours): (+44) (0)20 7930 4832 [This is the number on the Buckingham Palace website]
What you do for a living: Nothing
Do you own a house or rent apt: I rent from my wife
Have you lost money before: Yes, frequently
How much: Around £48 million but didn't count it exactly

How come you are born in 1921

Because that is when I was born.

Your Facebook says 5 July 1988.

I mistyped on Facebook and left it. It's difficult because I have NO HANDS.

OK
Your details has been confirmed and your name has been registered for CASH delivery and this is how you will get your money. You will now choose among the list of money below so that we can allocate the actual amount that will be deliver to you immediately.

Superb.

You have to pay for the Case file fee and the shipping fund that will authorise the delivery of your money immediately and we will bring your money to your door step by next day delivery.
Choose the money you want as follows and
Remember you can only choose once so choose wisely.

Great, just take the case file fee and the shipping money out of the LEATHER BRIEFCASE.
Also you should know my house has a gate so just slide it through the railings and I will have one of the staff COLLECT it.

You pay £1,500 and get £50,000.00 /

You pay £2,500 and get £140,000.00 /
You pay £3,000 and get £250,000.00 /
You pay £4,000 and get £450,000.00 /
You pay £6,000 and get £800,000.00 /
You pay £7,500 and get £2,000,000.00

The money you will send is the case file fund to clear your money and the private jet to take the money

Oh definitely £7,500 for £2,000,000.00, what a silly question – if it's in cash just take it now. Happy for you to take another £500 for your troubles.

You will need to send the money so that we can come for the delivery immediately.

There's no need because you have the money in the briefcase, so I am happy for you to just take it out of that.

We can't open it for security reason
Only the rightful owner can do that.

OK I understand. I will come to you. What is your nearest airport? One of my advisors will meet you on the runway.

We cannot say that information for security reason
Only the rightful owner can open no one else
You need to pay the case file and we bring to you.

Fair enough. How do I pay?

I will send you a secure link and all you do is enter bank card details.

I don't have a bank card.

Why don't you have bank card

Because I have NO HANDS. No I can only pay CASH or CHEQUE or PAYPAL.

The only way to pay is to use bank card.

OK I just found bank card.

OK what are the details

OK

5 4 3 2 1

I stopped there and didn't send him anything else. After an hour he replied.

What is the rest of the number?

No that is just a countdown to me sending you the number

OK send the number

I will send to you each number separately for security reasons

6

9

6

9

6

9

6

That's it.

Its not long enough number

OK maybe add another 9.

Bank card is 16 digit long

OK add 12345678.

Thats not a valid bank card.

I know. But you're not a valid human. This is a scam.

No I am acting on behalf of Mr Mark Zuckerberg and World Bank

Let me tell you who I am acting for. I work for the US Fraud Department and we have been tracing your messages. We can track everything about you. We know your name is not Bill Roberts. We know where you live. We are coming for you.

Whenever you see this picture. You know we're watching.

[Bill Roberts has left the conversation]

This is the only time each and every one of my aliases has come together to freak someone out. In succession, over a period of a few weeks, each one befriended Bill and sent him a picture of The Fox.

WE ARE STILL WATCHING.

[Bill Roberts has left the conversation]

Then another, from Paul Paulington:

WE HAVE EYES EVERYWHERE.

[Bill Roberts has left the conversation]

One from our beloved Paul Wenbridge:

WE WILL NEVER STOP.

[Bill Roberts has left the conversation]

And finally, Angie M.

ICH AM KOMING FOR YOU UND ICH HABE EIN MASSIVE LOAF AUF KNOBLAUCHBROT.

[Bill Roberts has left the conversation]

HOW I
WAS BEATEN BY
A CASINO

I am quite fond of a casino. Back when I worked as a front of house assistant in a theatre in Manchester, there was one nearby that I would frequent after my shifts, due to their policy of dishing out free sandwiches. The logic was that it would keep people in the premises and they'd then be tempted to gamble, but once I've had a sandwich I'd prefer a lie-down to frittering away my entire life savings. Also the sandwiches were appalling. 'Crisps sandwich' is not a thing.

A whole menagerie of late-night unusuals exist in casinos, from prostitutes to broken fathers, most of whom are lumbered with a troubling backstory that could easily make a *Coronation Street* subplot. Monthly earnings, mortgage repayments, children's inheritances, Nan's wallet contents – all of them are squandered here by someone who should know better. I am lucky when it comes to gambling, in that I am not lucky. I have profited less than £100 from casinos in my entire life and so there has been very little appeal to engage further. Although if you throw in the value of crisps sandwiches, then I am something of a millionaire. My favourite sort of gambling has always been those machines with a sliding metal tray covered in pennies. Why is it so satisfying just to watch gravity in action? They have now turned the concept into a whole TV show called *Tipping Point*, hosted by Ben Shephard, which I think may be the smartest move anyone has ever made in television. Making it into a TV show I mean, not Ben Shephard. Don't get me wrong, I like Ben Shephard but I once saw him throwing 2p pieces at a pigeon in Trafalgar Square and I've not been sure of him since.

The great benefit of a casino for me these days is that they serve alcohol twenty-four hours a day, so when I've been kicked out of a pub after last orders it is an ideal place to get in a final nightcap. Considering London is one of the major cities in the world, it has a frightful lack of late-night drinking establishments.

The most central casino is The Hippodrome, which used to be a theatre and is now a neon gambling hall with restaurants and bars around the perimeter. One evening I accompanied a friend to one of the blackjack tables, where she proceeded to haemorrhage about £50, shout profanities in anger and ultimately was asked to leave. Whilst she was totally in the wrong and the casino was absolutely within its rights to eject her, I promised her that I would destroy their business as vengeance for their rudeness/completely reasonable policy.

I considered complaining as myself but realised that would probably be ineffective. Casinos are all about money, and so I would need to talk to them in their language. Paul Wenbridge took on a new persona for the day, as an heir to a giant fortune with a petty attitude and time to kill. He sent this email.

To: *THE MANAGER*

I recently visited your casino and found it to be a shoddy establishment with an ugly interior and uglier patrons. What's more, my wife was left out in the cold as she was deemed unfit for your premises and I was robbed by the house.

I was and am so furious about my treatment in your casino that I am considering spending some of my considerable wealth on annoying you. I recently inherited hundreds of millions of pounds from my uncle, who passed away a few months ago. We were surprised at how rich he was but it appears that he invented a unique and ubiquitous type of bottle cap. I find wealth to be unappealing and I am a petty man with a lot of spare time, so rather than waste my uncle's money IN your casino, I feel that wasting it IRRITATING your casino may be preferable.

Some ways I may annoy you:

- Employ hundreds of dwarfs to stand outside your doors, shouting, 'We used to be tall before we gambled in this casino.'

- Release a van full of cats with gastroenteritis-induced diarrhoea onto your doorstep.

- Purchase neighbouring properties and turn them into casinos where the house always loses.

- Employ people to enter your casino undercover and release swarms of locusts at regular intervals.

- Bribe government officials to persuade them to change gambling laws to ones that will put you and your horrid premises out of business.

I should make it clear that I am not threatening to do this, I am just making it clear that, should I wish, I could do this. An apology from you may rectify the matter completely.

Regards,

Paul W

A week went by with no response. Alas, I thought this would be yet another email lost to the ether, never to be responded to or heard of again. Then, out of the blue, a glorious response spun into Mr Wenbridge's inbox.

Dear Sir,

Thank you for your letter concerning your experiences at The Hippodrome Casino. We have only been open 9 months and whilst already the busiest and most popular casino in the country, we appreciate any feedback, good or bad, recognising that there are bound to be areas that we can improve on.

Firstly your comments on the building. Many people love the interior and it is said to be one of the finest buildings designed by Frank Matcham over 100 years ago, but in any case it is listed, so we are limited in what we can do to it. As to our patrons, we are proud of all our customers; 'Beauty is in the eye of the beholder.'

Secondly, you say your wife was left out in the cold when you visited. Our sincere apologies for this. We shall immediately look to create a suitable refuge outside The Hippodrome for your wife on your next visit.

With regards to the numerous punishments that you have lined up for us and the use of your enormous wealth to carry them out:

The dwarfs: perhaps a little bad taste, given the history of dwarfs in the building. As you may know, when The Hippodrome opened over 100 years ago, it was an indoor circus with a large water tank in the middle of the ground floor. They had shows with elephants swimming in the tank, and other shows with dwarfs high-diving from the Minstrels Gallery 60 ft above the water tank. All went well until they tried to combine the shows and the rest is history, certainly for two of the dwarfs anyway. But in any case, if you get an army of dwarfs, we would have no choice but to get our own *army of dwarfs to combat them, and we could have a 'small' battle in Cranbourne St.*

The cats: please don't, we have only just got rid of the last lot.

The neighbouring property route: we like this idea, so please go ahead; it will give customers more money to come and enjoy themselves with at The Hippodrome, which is by far the best property in the area.

Your locusts: it makes us smile just thinking about the poor chaps coming in with a swarm of locusts under their coats. It could be a tad uncomfortable for them.

Government officials: any chance of getting the government officials to carry the locusts in? It would make us smile even more.

So, in short, we would dread to think of you carrying out any of your ingenious plots, and naturally unreservedly apologise for any offence caused, knowingly or unknowingly. Please do introduce yourself on your next visit (with or without wife); we will make sure you are well looked after and will happily buy you a drink for the pleasure you have given us.

Yours sincerely,

Paul Mettam

What an absolute badass.

Paul Wenbridge was put firmly in his place there and, by Paul Wenbridge, I of course mean me. I sent a response threatening I would turn up on a random date to claim my free drink. It was in vain: he didn't reply. Why would he? He's already won. I licked my wounds and decided to leave the matter alone. I had been defeated. It got a few laughs as a routine in my stand-up and I was happy with that.

What happened next, I am yet to fully comprehend. A friend

of mine who had heard the story sent me a cryptic text: 'Get a copy of the *Metro*. Look at the General Appointments section.' Fortunately, I was in London Euston at the time and you are never more than 2 cm away from a 30p toilet or a copy of the *Metro* there. What I found baffled me beyond belief:

I had to read it a few times to fully absorb it. The Hippodrome were actively ADVERTISING FOR DOOR DWARFS. This must be The Hippodrome's final twist of the knife, a kick in the teeth, a tour de force. Not content with taking my stupid email and spinning it against me with wit and sass, they had now dug in deeper, taken my idea and run with it. I've never known defeat like it.

I suppose, in the end, however much you try to convince yourself otherwise, the cliché is true: the house always wins.

SO ANNOYING WHEN YOU
MEAN TO TEXT 'HEY HOW ARE YOU'

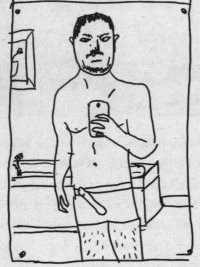

BUT IT AUTO CORRECTS TO
A SELFIE WITH YOU ERECT
IN THE BATHROOM MIRROR.

GLOSSARY
OF UNACCEPTABLE
WORDS & PHRASES

Considering email has been around for only a relatively short amount of time*, it is surprising to note how many traditions and habits have formed in frequent users. We have become so normalised to email and digital contact that we have allowed certain undesirable tendencies to thrive. We all know the correct etiquette in real life – look people in the eye, shake their hand, avoid genital contact on first meeting. But what is the code of conduct for Internet communications?

There are a number of words and phrases in common usage in today's emails that I consider to be completely unacceptable.

---

* *Relative to the age of the universe, not to my age, which is 28, unless you work in showbusiness, and then it's 12.*

Many of these will be familiar to you and, as such, perhaps you think they are perfectly fine. You are mistaken. If I catch any of you using them, I will put you on my list. I can't say what will happen to people on my list, but it involves a bird bath filled with old pesto and repeated episodes of *Geordie Shore*. You've been warned.

Here is an exhaustive, (by exhaustive, I don't mean comprehensive, just that I find them exhausting) list of irksome terms that you must avoid. I also recommend refusing to have any contact with anyone who litters your inbox with these contemptible vagaries:

SOON

Example: 'I'll have a response to you soon.'

The word 'soon' is relative. You could argue that a Mars-sized object smashed into the earth and 'soon' after the moon was formed, but this gap in time was about 10 million years. 10 million years is pretty soon in relation to the age of the universe, but not very soon if that's how long you're waiting for a tax rebate.

SOMEONE

Example: 'Someone from the technical team will be in touch tomorrow.'

In a hostage situation this word can be very powerful, because it's so vague that it creates terror, such as in sentences like, 'Every hour you don't meet my demands, someone will die.'

SHOULD

Example: 'Martin should be back to you by the end of the week.'

What kind of life is Martin living where he cannot estimate

whether he is capable of responding to an email within a week? Are Martin's time resources so difficult to predict? No. Martin works in the complaints department at John Lewis and he will get back to me by the end of the week or he shouldn't be surprised if I send him abusive, suspicious-smelling letters in the mail.

END OF PLAY

Example: 'I'll have the documents to you by end of play Tuesday.'

Your end of play is different to my end of play. I never stop playing. I work hard and party harder. Give me a specific time, please. Also, you can't describe working in a South Birmingham solicitors as 'play'.

HOPE YOU'RE WELL

Example: 'The fine for this illegal parking is £65. Hope you're well.'

So many people put this at the end of their emails because they have nothing more creative to end on and I have honestly received it at least half a dozen times after messages with bad news. NO, I AM NOT WELL, I HAVE JUST BEEN FINED £65.

APOLOGIES FOR THE DELAY

Example: 'Apologies for the delay in replying, it's been crazy busy.'

It has not been 'crazy busy' – you have been 'crazy lazy'. Your apology is worthless.

PLEASE DON'T HESITATE

Example: 'Please don't hesitate to send me any further questions.'

Why would I hesitate? I never hesitate. I act on instinct always, capable of lashing out without a moment's notice. I am a spontaneous, fluid spirit who will not waste a second before asking you what council tax band I am in.

WORD DOCUMENT
Example: 'I'll send you the information in a Word document.'
Spare me. Word documents are a niche form of intense torture. Please just do us all a favour, and copy and paste the text into the email and avoid me having to go on a killing spree.

OUT OF OFFICE
Example: 'I am out of the office until next Wednesday so will be unable to respond to your email before then.'
You are a liar. The whole point of email is that it is accessible as long as you have a smartphone and you have access to 3G or wi-fi, which is literally anywhere. I would accept this ONLY if you don't have Internet access because you are in a Third World country, but I don't think that's the case because your Facebook just updated to say you have bought a new cow on FarmVille. ANSWER. MY. EMAIL.

NB: There is a loophole in the rules that states that one person is allowed to use the above words and phrases. That person is me and I use them all on a frequent basis. If you want to complain about it, please don't hesitate to send me your thoughts in a Word document and soon someone should send you a response by the end of play on one of the days in the future. Apologies for the delay but I can't respond as I'm out of the office. Hope you're well! xxx

GENERAL TIPS

Whilst I have attempted to impart all the wisdom you should ever need upon these pages, there may be some issues that I have failed to resolve. To make amends, please find here a list of some generic activities you can enjoy to lash out passive-aggressively at those who have irked you.

SUBSCRIBE THEM TO AN INAPPROPRIATE MAGAZINE

If they're married, why not subscribe them to a light pornographic magazine or indulge in a hardcore publication for extra awkwardness? If they're a homophobic alpha male a six-month subscription to *Gay Times* should do the trick.

PAY FOR A SKIP TO BE PLACED OUTSIDE THEIR HOUSE

When my friend bought her first house, it took the owners over twelve months to vacate it. For the last three, she paid for a skip to be put outside simply to annoy them. It also came in handy when she actually wanted to get rid of their ugly leftover furniture/fresh corpses.

ADD GLITTER TO ALL ENVELOPES

A simple trick that worked beautifully with my friend who sent me hate mail, glitter is one of life's most fantastically infuriating inventions. Apply liberally. Be careful when you open their reply, in case they've sent it back (like my bank did once).

SIGN THEIR EMAIL ADDRESS UP TO AS MANY MAILING LISTS AS POSSIBLE

The more the better. I find the most annoying ones are all airlines and change.org.

TIP OFF HMRC THAT THEY'RE NOT PAYING THEIR TAX

You can ring HMRC anonymously with a 'tip-off', which they are then obliged to investigate. An investigation by HMRC is apparently one of the most arduous and stressful things in an adult's life, akin to childbirth or watching an episode of *This Morning* when Amanda Holden is hosting.

SEND THEM 500 COPIES OF THIS BOOK

It'll be a nightmare to find storage for them all and you'll be doing me a real favour.

STAND OUTSIDE THEIR HOUSE CHANTING BIBLICAL PHRASES

This can really spook them out and is a great afternoon activity with the kids!

DRAFT FAKE LETTERS FROM THEIR DOCTOR

The NHS logo is easily available online – whack it on the top of a letter and then write something like, 'My apologies for writing to you without warning, but we have found some old test results of yours that show something very, very worrying and we need you to come in as soon as possible.' Put some glitter in the envelope, sit back and relax.

FOLLOW THEM WITH A KNIFE

I find this one is really effective!!!

If none of these work, then you are probably dealing with someone very powerful or you're trying to annoy me. Also, I'm not sure but I think some of these might be illegal, so don't sue me if you end up in jail!

ACKNOWLEDGEMENTS

Thanks first and foremost to Hannah Black, my editor, Vero, Liz and all at Hodder, who have been so encouraging and positive about what is a frankly ridiculous book for anyone to publish.

To my agent Hannah Chambers and everyone at Chambers Management who are the absolute best people you are likely to meet and who coordinate my entire life with ease and calm.

To all at my PR Multitude Media, particularly my dear old friend Will Wood for being the wisest man in the world.

To my mother, father and sister, Beth for their love and encouragement and nodding along when I've told them my numerous ludicrous ideas and plans.

To Amie for her million little encouragements and celebrations as I've written this.

To David Charles for first introducing me to the phrase 'doth butter no parsnips'. Plus to Jenny Beavan, Caitlin Albery Beavan and all at the Asylum, who are a constant support and inspiration.

To Karen Bayley and Eleanor Thom, for reading drafts and making this much funnier.

To Sarah King, for her constant belief and friendship from the start.

To my friend and mentor Edward Stambollouian, who has patiently pushed me to be better when I've been lazy, which is always.

To the women in comedy who have supported me endlessly: Sarah Millican, Katherine Ryan (and Violet), Aisling Bea, Sara Pascoe, Bridget Christie, Isy Suttie, Janice Connolly, Lou Sanders and Susan Calman.

To Jimmy, Sean, Jon, Susie and Rachel and everyone at *8 Out of 10 Cats Does Countdown*, who have always encouraged me to go further with this madness.

To my Birmingham pals, everyone in the Best of Brum Love WhatsApp group (Ahmad, Andy, Caroline, Carter, Claud, Cuong, Fern, Jimbob, Joe, Josephine, Kad, Larry, Lee, Matty, Rachel, Sarah P, Scrim, Ste, Steph, Zubair), who always come and support me, even though they've heard the jokes a million times. Plus shout out to Digbeth.

To Richard 'Tango' Simpson, who first showed me how to be really daft.

To Simon Longman and Ed Franklin, for their inspiration back in the Salford days, most notably 'Cluttons'.

To Matt Crockett for, amongst other things, 'I'm Syrious.'

To Sarah Churchwell, for imparting her considerable wisdom about writing and publishing.

To Aidan Butler, James Kettle and Zac Fox.

Biggest thanks to all the people who I've emailed over the years. Even if you didn't give permission and we had to change your name, I still think you're the best.

Sorry if I forgot to put you on this list, but it's probably 'cause I think you're a knob.

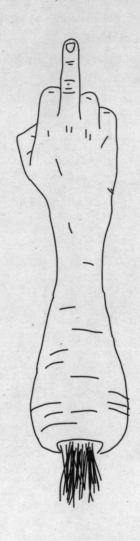